ERIC SEALS

MORRIS PETERSON AND MATEEN CLEAVES SHARE A SHINING MOMENT DURING MICHIGAN STATE'S NCAA TOURNAMENT RUN.

Contents

DAVID P. GILKEY

TOM IZZO HAD THE SPARTANS POINTED IN THE RIGHT DIRECTION AFTER WINNING THE BIG TEN TOURNAMENT. ON THE COVER: WITH THE JOB COMPLETE, MATEEN CLEAVES AND THE SPARTANS WERE NO. 1.

Our team

Tom Panzenhagen — Editor

Brian James — Designer

Ken Kraemer — Copy chief

Alan R. Kamuda — Photo editor

Bob Ellis — Technical support

Doug Church — Sixth man

Christine Russell — Photo lab tech

Special thanks to Steve Anderson, Bill Collison, Steve Dorsey, Robert Kozloff, Tim Marcinkoski, Gene Myers, Dave Robinson, Shelly Solon, Kelly Solon, Laura Varon and the Free Press sports staff.

Cover photo by Eric Seals.

Detroit Free Press

TRIUMPH

© Detroit Free Press and Triumph Books.
All rights reserved.

No part of this publication may be reproduced, stored in a retrieval system or transmitted, in any form or by any means, electronic, mechanical, photocopying or otherwise, without the prior written consent of the publisher, Triumph Books, 601 South LaSalle Street, Suite 500, Chicago, Ill. 60605. Manufactured by Quad/Graphics.

Detroit Free Press, 600 W. Fort, Detroit, Mich. 48226
To subscribe to the Free Press call 1-800-395-3300.
Find the Freep on the World Wide Web at www.freep.com

Other recent books by the Free Press sports staff:
Corner to Copa   Century of Champions
The Corner   Believe!
M1CH1GAN   Stanleytown
To order, call 800-245-5082 or go to www.freep.com/bookstore

ISBN 1-57243-372-8

How often do three kids from the same neighborhood grow up together,
go to school together and win a national championship together?

THEY YABBA DABBA DID IT

BY MITCH ALBOM

When he couldn't fly, he fell. When he couldn't stand, he crawled. When he couldn't take the pain, he took it because you only get one night like this in your life, if you're lucky, and you'll take a bullet in the leg if you can get back out there and win. Mateen Cleaves knew it. His Michigan State teammates knew it. And so, after soaring on a crazy, flying layup, tangling legs with Florida's Teddy Dupay as he came down and twisting his ankle so badly the crowd winced in unison, after crying out in pain and crawling toward his bench, after disappearing into the locker room with the biggest question mark of the college basketball season hanging over his head, Mateen Cleaves was coming back out onto the floor in the championship game at Indianapolis, with his team clinging desperately to its lead over Florida.

And before he stepped on the court, he did what they all had been doing. He turned to that sea of green across from the Spartans' bench. You look homeward when you need your strength, and after every big moment in this championship game, that is what the Spartans did. Looked across this sold-out RCA Dome to see their mothers, fathers, sisters, brothers, aunts, uncles, cousins and alumni, to see Magic Johnson, Steve Smith, Jud Heathcote, to see the grandpas of the past and the little brothers of the future never letting up, sending the Spartans strength, urging them to fulfill their destiny that began five months earlier and was culminating in the biggest game of their lives.

"I told the trainer that they were going to have to amputate my leg to keep me out of this one," Cleaves would say.

The ref beckoned him back and Cleaves stepped onto the court, tattoo on his arm, heart on his sleeve.

And now he has a ring on his finger.

"Was it worth coming back for your senior year?" someone asked Cleaves after Michigan State's inspiring 89-76 victory over Florida for the national championship.

"Worth it?" Cleaves yelled. "Oh my God! This is what I came back for!"

The perfect night. The perfect finish to his career and his senior teammates. The perfect climax for the team that Tom Izzo began to build when he took over the program in 1995.

Here was a championship that showed that three senior starters are worth their weight in gold, that defense and rebounding still beat fast breaks and a breathless press, that nothing you do in a season goes wasted because, had Michigan State not played the first 13 games of the year without Cleaves, sidelined with a broken foot, they might never have held such poise in the title game.

But mostly, this was a night that showed what happens when you trust your roots.

So it was Charlie Bell, being ripped into the air and dropped like a paper bag by Florida's huge Donnell Harvey. Bell drew the foul, got up and stared into that special section of the crowd, his face a picture of intensity.

It was Morris Peterson spinning into the lane, banging off a body and twisting for a lay-up. He, too, looked

to that section, nodded his head, as if to say, "It's coming, it's coming, everything we dreamed of."

It was A. J. Granger — the unsung hero of the night, with 19 points and nine rebounds — hitting a three-pointer, and despite his understated personality, almost waving a fist at his family.

And it was Cleaves, who couldn't shoot or cut or even run full speed after the high-ankle sprain, somehow managing to get the ball to the right people, dishing to Peterson for lay-ups, even ripping down a rebound and looking, once again, to the source of his strength.

The green, green crowd of home.

"WE'RE COMING HOME, MICHIGAN STATE!" he yelled. "WE'RE COMING HOME, FLINT!"

Home. You see? Because they never forgot where they came from, they have become what they are.

Champions of the nation.

What a game. The first half was a flying circus, barely time to breathe. The Florida press was supposed to trip up Michigan State, the experts said, the way gnats around your eyes can make you lose your reading concentration. What the experts forgot — or, more likely, never knew — is that State loves to run far more than it likes to bang.

So here was pass city, Granger-to-Bell-to-Andre Hutson-to-Cleaves outside for a three-pointer. Net! Cleaves-to-Peterson-to-a-streaking-Granger down the lane. Dunk! Bell off a steal to Jason Richardson-to-Bell-to-Richardson for a fast break. Lay-up! It was faster than hockey, and the numbers fell like pinball. In less than 10 minutes, the Spartans had 21 points, exceeding their total first-half output against Wisconsin in the semifinal.

But all this seemed meaningless just under four minutes into the second half, when Cleaves went down and began his sad crawl to the bench. The Spartans led by only six points, and Cleaves had scored 18. He clearly had been the best player out there.

"Yeah, I was worried," Izzo admitted afterward, "because Mateen is not the kind of guy who fakes an injury to get sympathy from his girlfriend. But once I saw it wasn't broken, I told Mateen, 'OK, you have a few minutes to get it taped and then get back out here.' And he said he would."

In the meantime, the Spartans went on, the way they have in the face of adversity all season long. Mike Chappell, the transfer from Duke who struggled all year, hit five straight points, the biggest five points of his MSU career. And Granger pulled up for a three-pointer. And Peterson — Cleaves' best friend and roommate — kept scoring and scoring, 15 points in the second half.

The whole team pulled together, and by the time Cleaves came hobbling back out, the lead not only had held but had grown to nine points.

The game was won. It just needed to be finished.

And so, finally, after what Izzo called "a bull's-eye on our back all year," the Spartans got to climb that ladder and cut down the nets. And as they took their pieces of thread, they turned to the crowd as if to share every strand.

This piece of net goes to Flint, a city that has been on the canvas for so long, it almost has gotten used to being down. But this little victory can change that. You don't save a city with a sports team, but you begin to save one with pride, and the championship was a cleansing rinse. Cleaves, Peterson, Bell — and Antonio Smith, who almost did

ERIC SEALS

THE NATIONAL CHAMPIONSHIP BROUGHT JOY TO A PAIR OF PLAYERS WHO HELPED FORM THE BEDROCK OF THE TEAM: CHARLIE BELL AND MORRIS PETERSON.

it with last year's team — will never forget their hometown. And it will never forget them.

This piece of net goes to Izzo, who did things the right way. He waited his turn until Heathcote retired. He built his program. He didn't go flying all over the country, taking this gig, that gig, this glitter, that glitter. Plenty has been made of where Izzo was born — Iron Mountain — but not enough has been

ERIC SEALS

Sparty hearty — from left: Mat Ishbia, Charlie Bell, Tom Izzo and Mateen Cleaves raise the roof in Indianapolis.

made about where he stayed. Namely, the state of Michigan — his whole career. The only surprise with Izzo is that he isn't shaped like a hand.

And this piece of net goes to Spartans fans, who, let's face it, have had their faces rubbed in Michigan's success for long enough. When U-M won the 1989 championship, MSU fans kept saying, "Remember 1979." And when U-M outrecruited MSU for Chris Webber and Jalen Rose, then the two best players in the state, MSU kept saying, "Remember 1979." And when Steve Fisher's Fab Five went to two straight national championship games, MSU kept saying, "Remember 1979."

That 1979 championship became the crumpled photo that the GI keeps in the foxhole. The memory is strong, but, as time passes, you wonder whether you'll ever feel the embrace again.

See those fans hugging one another? That's a pretty strong embrace, isn't it?

And so, finally, MSU fans get to say, "Move over, Magic." This 2000 team will be remembered for so many things, for Granger's growth into a major shooting force, for Bell's tremendous defense and rebounding, for Hutson's unsung strength and bravery in the middle against every big man they could throw at him.

And, of course, for the Flintstones — Cleaves, Peterson, Bell. How often do three kids from the same neighborhood grow up together, go to school together and win a national championship together?

"I want to cherish this moment forever," Peterson said. "It really hasn't hit me that this is the last game I'll ever play as a Spartan. . . . I guess this is the perfect ending."

He smiled and fingered the large hunk of net that hung around his neck.

"I'm going to give some pieces of this to my family, but the rest I'm going to wear." He smiled. "Yeah. I'm going to wear this around my neck for the next three days."

What is the most impressive part of this team? That the Spartans were the only No. 1 seed to make the Final Four? That they were the only No. 1 seed to have to face a No. 2 seed? That they came from behind in three of the six tournament games? That they shrugged off the Florida press as if they'd played it a thousand times? That they shot 55.9 percent and scored 89 points on a championship night when nerves are supposed to ruin your accuracy?

What was most impressive?

It's all impressive.

And perhaps this last scene is most impressive of all: With moments left in the game, and the outcome decided, Cleaves began to dance.

Dance? Yep. The same guy who began the season with a broken foot, who missed part of the last game with a terribly twisted ankle, and here he was dancing in place, a smile as big as Disneyland. What did Sparky Anderson once say, "Pain don't hurt"?

Not when you win.

"I LOVE YOU, MICHIGAN STATE!" he yelled.

They love him back.

Tattoos on their arms, hearts on their sleeves and rings on their fingers. Paint the state and mark the calendar. The team that did it the right way is returning to the green, green grass of home.

With a trophy.

AFTER THEY DISSECTED MICHIGAN BY 51 POINTS IN THE REGULAR-SEASON FINALE, THE
SPARTANS' NET RESULT WAS A SHARE OF THEIR THIRD STRAIGHT BIG TEN TITLE.

The Spartans made a vow after their loss to Duke ...

'WE'LL BE BACK'

JULIAN H. GONZALEZ

AT THE END OF THE IMPROBABLE TITLE RUN, TOM IZZO PONDERS HIS NEXT GOAL: "WE HAVE TO GET TO THE FINAL FOUR NEXT YEAR."

MSU FANS WHO WORE THIS T-SHIRT WERE READY TO PUT UP THEIR DUKES.

BY JEMELE HILL

Soon after the Spartans lost to Duke in the 1999 national semifinals, Michigan State associate coach Tom Crean walked onto the court at Tropicana Field in St. Petersburg, Fla., and kissed the Final Four logo.

"People doubted us, but we got here, baby," Crean said. "We'll be back."

The Spartans had been eliminated, but they weren't defeated.

"I'm really looking forward to trying to get back," Tom Izzo said after Duke ended MSU's championship run, 68-62. "As far as how we will do it, I don't know. I think we have good players coming back."

Few thought the 1998-99 Spartans would go so far. "Us Against the World" had become their motto.

"One thing I'm proud about is that

JULIAN H. GONZALEZ

WHAT MIGHT HAVE BEEN: WILLIAM AVERY WHOOPS IT UP AFTER DUKE'S SEMIFINAL VICTORY.

people were down on us and we always believed in ourselves," Morris Peterson said. "We always gave 110 percent when we stepped onto the basketball court."

The worker-bee attitude produced record-setting results: The Spartans finished 33-5, the most victories in Big Ten history, and they won a school-best 22 straight games. The Spartans won the regular season and tournament championships, finishing 18-1 against conference opponents.

"It's been a great year," said senior forward Antonio Smith, who departed with 1,016 rebounds — only the third player in team history to top 1,000.

It was the year Izzo laid the groundwork for MSU to be ranked alongside the nation's elite teams. When the season was over, fans knew they wouldn't have to wait another 20 years to see the Spartans go far in the Big Dance.

Izzo's goal for 2000 was clear: "We have to get to the Final Four next year."

A season up in smoke

FREE PRESS STAFF AND NEWS SERVICES

A riotous crowd of about 5,000 people threw bottles and started fires around an apartment complex close to the Michigan State campus shortly after the Spartans lost to Duke in the Final Four.

"They're starting fires wherever there is anything they can burn," East Lansing deputy fire chief Pete Zamora said. There were reports of Dumpsters, sofas and a car being set ablaze.

Zamora said there were numerous injuries, mostly people who were cut by thrown bottles. One person was climbing a traffic light pole and fell. Another was burned while jumping over a flaming sofa.

One police officer was injured. In the aftermath, the following numbers were reported:

■ 230 police officers on the scene from 12 departments.

■ 61 fires set.

■ 29 people treated at Sparrow Hospital.

■ 24 arrests.

Campus police Capt. Tony Kliebecker said the department sent its riot unit in to quell the crowd that had gathered around the Cedar Village apartment complex.

He said police sprayed tear gas to try to disperse the crowd so firefighters could get to a car that had been overturned and set on fire.

East Lansing fire marshal Bob Pratt said firefighters were pulling back at Cedar Village because they were being pelted with debris. Zamora said one fire truck windshield was broken by thrown debris.

"This is pathetic," said Mark Berry, a sophomore at the school. "They're just tearing the campus apart."

News of the rioting disgusted Tom Izzo. "Everything we did this season," he said, the rioters "undid to a certain extent.

"I've never been more angry or embarrassed about anything in my years at Michigan State. And if any of them are watching me right now, and if they're students or fans of Michigan State basketball, I don't want you as a part of my program any longer.

"If you're a season-ticket holder, I will personally buy your tickets next year because I don't want you as a fan. I don't want you in the building. I don't want you as a part of my program. I don't understand that kind of behavior.

"We try to give them something to be proud about, something to be happy about, and this is how they thank us.... What happened was ridiculous. It was sick."

ERIC SEALS

THE BURNING QUESTION IN EAST LANSING WAS HOW COULD SOMETHING LIKE THIS HAPPEN?

We need you to finish the job ...

COME BACK, MATEEN

DEAR MATEEN:

Don't even think about it. I know the NBA is out there. I know certain friends and relatives will be whispering in your ear now, saying you can make it big, cash in, get paid for playing basketball instead of giving it away for free.

Tell them thanks, but no thanks. Now is not the time to go.

This has nothing to do with talent. You have plenty of talent. You have enough to be drafted into the NBA, which already puts you in the most elite level of basketball on the planet. Whether your talent is polished enough to be a lottery pick — in my opinion it is not there yet — that shouldn't be the issue.

The issue should be that locker room you left at the Final Four.

Remember the scene?

It was quiet and subdued. In one corner was senior Antonio Smith, your soul mate, your fellow Flintstone. He had just played his last game for MSU. His career was over, one game short of the national championship. When he fouled out, with 16 seconds left, he walked off slowly, a bit dazed, as if someone had clunked him over the head with a brick. That's because his time was up.

And he couldn't do a thing about it.

In another corner was Jason Klein, another senior. He sat slumped in his chair, looking at his feet. He'd missed several open jumpers that could have pushed your team even with Duke. He was replaying them in his head, over and over, you could see the images spinning behind his unfocused eyes.

"Right now, if you could come back for another year — even if you had to take a full load of classes — would you do it?" he was asked.

"Oh, absolutely," he said. "No question."

You know why? His dreams were plucked too soon. And he, too, couldn't do a thing about it.

But you can.

Remember how you said after the game, "Something touched me inside when I watched Antonio and Jason and TK (Thomas Kelley) walk off. It was sad. They'll never wear the Spartan green again."

You can wear it. You can grab that green baton, come back next year and lead this team on a quest to capture the only thing you didn't in 1999, a national title.

You should do it. Not because I say so, or because MSU fans say so, or even because your coach, Tom Izzo, says so. You should do it because you have the chance. It doesn't come very often.

Older champions always talk of how they were formed by winning a title. The sweat, the faith, the relentless dedication, it all stays with them long after they stop shooting jumpers. It affects who they are. It molds their personalities. Look at Magic Johnson, your guardian angel. His winning is all over his face.

You have a chance at that. You won a title in high school. That's good. Maybe you'll join a championship NBA franchise — odds are you won't. But this Spartans team could be great next year.

Morris Peterson, your leading scorer, is coming back. A. J. Granger, the long-range surprise of the postseason, is coming back. Charlie Bell and Andre Hutson, both starters, are coming back. Then there's hugely talented Mike Chappell, the Duke transfer who had to sit out this season. And a crop of gifted backups

and promising recruits.

All this, in a program that already reached the national semifinals and is finally getting its due. Surely you noticed, in the last few weeks, how people outside of East Lansing were saying "Mateen" and "Antonio" and "MoPete" as if they knew them. The Spartans became the state's team during this tournament.

It's taken 20 years, but it's not just about Michigan, Fab Five or maize and blue anymore. It's about green now. Not as a second choice. As a preference. You've helped set the mold. You can help cement it. If you come back.

And yet even that isn't the biggest reason. The biggest reason is in the laughs, the hugs and the practical jokes that come with being part of a team. It's that huddle that you guys form before the game, arm in arm, like the comrades that you are. It's in the college nicknames. It's in the late-night pizza sessions. It's in the tattoos that say Flint, your hometown, where you and so many of your teammates were forged.

Trust me. You won't be tattooing the name of your NBA team on your arm. You said it yourself after the Duke game. "These guys are my family." That's worth a lot. I can't tell you how many NBA players who jumped out early have told me later how they wished they'd stayed.

Just as I can't tell you how many college juniors have said — as you did after the game — "I'm planning to come back, but I have to sit down with Coach and my family and see what's best."

They say that and, a month later, they're standing with an agent at a press conference, announcing their departure. I don't believe you will do that. I think you're too smart. I think Coach Izzo will tell you even his NBA

"Something touched me inside when I watched Antonio and Jason and TK (Thomas Kelley) walk off. It was sad. They'll never wear the Spartan green again."

MATEEN CLEAVES

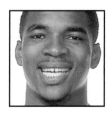

SMITH

KLEIN

KELLEY

connections suggest one more year.

But there will be a lonesome moment, I'm sure, when you wonder, "What if I went?"

Don't do it. Stay. You're too spe-cial. You have too unique a chance. You'll end up making more money from the NBA the following year. And, besides, while you shouldn't lis-ten to me, the fans or even necessar-ily your coach, you should always lis-ten to one person.

Your Mom.

She wants you to stay, too.

See you in September.

SPARTYKISS!
THIS POSTGAME
PALACE EMBRACE
BETWEEN MATEEN
AND FRANCES
CLEAVES WAS A
MOMENT OF
PRIDE AND JOY
NEAR THE END
OF A LONG AND
HAPPY ROAD.

ERIC SEALS

Money isn't everything – Cleaves says, "I'm staying"

HAPPY MOTHER'S DAY

BY DREW SHARP

Mother's Day came three days early for Frances Cleaves. The best gift she could imagine came in the form of two simple words:

"I'm staying."

Her son Mateen's decision to put off the NBA for another year was worth a house full of cards, flowers and candy.

"Mateen's father and I truly got involved in the process," Frances Cleaves said. "I didn't know that the parents could contact the teams themselves until the NCAA told us we could. So I got on the phone and got as much information as I could. Mo (Mateen) could trust me more than he could trust any agent.

"You have no idea of how proud I am of my Mateen," she said. "There was a lot of pressure on him to leave — and it came from everywhere. Friends back in Flint were telling him that he should take the money now because, even though it wouldn't be as much as he could get next year, it's still more money than any of us ever imagined."

But Frances Cleaves spoke of riches that can't be computed in a checkbook. And Mateen Cleaves made a bold statement one hopes will resonate through the playgrounds of Flint: There is virtue in putting academics ahead of athletics.

"We don't like to admit it at times, but we are role models as athletes," Cleaves said. "People might have a hard time believing why I would turn down the chance to make that kind of money. But I'm having fun here at Michigan State. Why should I give that up when I don't have to?"

The best-laid plans ...

BY JEMELE HILL

ERIC SEALS

WE'VE COME A LONG WAY, BABY. FRANCES CLEAVES, MATEEN'S MOM, CHEERED THE SPARTANS' MIDWEST REGIONAL WIN OVER IOWA STATE AT THE PALACE. THE SEASON DIDN'T BEGIN WITH JOY FOR MATEEN, HOWEVER.

Mateen Cleaves, who was diagnosed with a stress fracture in his right foot, was told he would miss the first half of the season.

"This is a big blow to our team and program," Tom Izzo said. "I think we'll find out, do we have a team or do we have a program?"

The Spartans weren't sure what caused the injury. Stress fractures often result from wear and tear.

"The guy is down about what happened," Izzo said. "It's been a traumatic day. He's worked so hard. I've been told that life is not fair, and this is one of those times I believe it."

Though Cleaves would attend all games and practices, MSU wouldn't have its emotional leader. "That will be the hardest thing to find," Izzo said. "He's our leader by his actions and words. He's just going to be a very talented assistant for 10 weeks."

WILLIAM ARCHIE

A STRESS FRACTURE IN HIS RIGHT FOOT PUT MATEEN CLEAVES ON CRUTCHES AND OUT OF THE LINEUP UNTIL JAN. 5.

Coaches corner

OPENING STUFF

No Cleaves? No problem vs. Rockets

Best buddies since their high school days in Iron Mountain, Tom Izzo and Steve Mariucci have shared their dreams. Now they were sharing nightmares. Both coaches were without their quarterbacks.

Mariucci, the coach of the San Francisco 49ers, was missing Steve Young because of a concussion. Izzo was without Mateen Cleaves because of a stress fracture in his right foot.

"We've talked a lot about what you can do, and what you have to, when you lose your best player," Izzo said. "It's not easy because you find out how everything revolves around that player. Steve's finding that out now. You take a Steve Young out of the mix, and look what that does to not just the offense but the attitude of that entire team."

Fortunately for the Spartans, they were playing the Toledo Rockets and not the St. Louis Rams.

ANDRE HUTSON BEGAN THE LONG ROAD BACK TO THE FINAL FOUR WITH AN EXCLAMATION POINT AGAINST TOLEDO IN THE OPENER.

Associated Press photos

MATEEN CLEAVES MADE THE BEST OF HIS SUPPORTING ROLE AGAINST TOLEDO AND IN THE FOLLOWING 12 GAMES.

BY JEMELE HILL

Michigan State might not have its All-America point guard, but as long as MSU plays well defensively, Tom Izzo hopes the Spartans can weather the absence.

A strong defensive effort overpowered Toledo, 78-33, on opening night at the Breslin Center. Disappointed with his team's effort in exhibitions, Izzo saw a friskier, defensive-minded team.

"I thought we played a lot harder than we did the last time out," Izzo said. "We didn't give up very many shots, and we did a good job of cutting off the penetration other than for a few possessions. We won the game by defending and rebounding. Spartan basketball — to me — is what you saw."

Morris Peterson and Andre Hutson carried the scoring bulk. Hutson, a quiet offensive performer in 1998-99, scored 15 points and tied a career high with 10 rebounds. Peterson scored 19 points on 8-for-12 shooting from the floor and had 10 rebounds.

"We've asked him to take over," Izzo said of Peterson. "You'll see him handle the ball more. I was very pleased with a lot of things he did tonight."

THE STRESS BEGINS TO SHOW

RICARDO FIGUEROA/Associated Press

CHARLIE BELL AND ANDRE HUTSON BATTLE TEXAS' CHRIS MIHM DURING A LOSS THAT TYPIFIED THE IMPACT OF MATEEN CLEAVES' ABSENCE.

BY JEMELE HILL

There were two ways to look at Michigan State's experience in the Puerto Rico Shootout — either as a growing experience, or more proof that the Spartans desperately needed leader Mateen Cleaves, who was recovering from a stress fracture in his right foot.

Either way, the facts weren't positive. The Spartans blew double-digit leads in the semifinal and championship games, easing up on teams they could have buried. MSU outlasted South Carolina, 59-56, but was upset in the final by No. 20 Texas, 81-74.

"Once you get up on a team early, you get a sense it will be an easy game," said Charlie Bell, who was selected to the all-tournament team. "But once we get teams down, we just have to bury them because we have a target on our back."

The Spartans played nearly flawless basketball in building first-half leads of 13 points against the Gamecocks and 15 against the Longhorns. But that intensity was missing in the second half of both games.

"Sometimes when you're ranked this high (No. 3), you think you're better than you are," said Morris Peterson, who also was selected to the all-tournament team. "We have to understand that if we don't do the little things, we'll lose the game. We need to sacrifice ourselves, get floor burns to get the intensity."

The Spartans' dogged defensive tenacity was missing against Texas, which made 7-of-9 three-point attempts in the second half, when preseason All-America center Chris Mihm had 12 points and seven rebounds.

"I thought we played hard enough to win a game like that," Tom Izzo said. "But we didn't do the job defensively in the second half."

The Spartans would have to learn from their mistakes, and quickly. Coming up were even tougher opponents — North Carolina, Kansas, Arizona, and Kentucky — before the new year.

Spartans pull off
an upset, dedicate
it to football team

IZZO: THIS ONE'S FOR THEM

BY DREW SHARP

It was a big moment for Michigan State basketball, yet Tom Izzo went on national television and dedicated the victory over North Carolina to the Michigan State football team.

"This one's for them," Izzo said.

Nick Saban's abrupt departure for LSU affirmed what many already believed — Izzo is the poster boy of Michigan State athletics. Before the basketball team left for the game in North Carolina, Izzo talked to the football team, still dazed over the loss of its head coach.

Izzo asked the team to gather together to watch his hoopsters meet the challenge of facing the nation's No. 2 team on its home floor. He also talked about toughness and perseverance.

Sounds like his basketball team listened as well.

Non-conference opponents don't come into the Dean Smith Center expecting much good fortune. The Tar Heels had a 55-game non-conference home winning streak and a winning streak in home openers that dated to 1928.

That is, until Morris Peterson came calling. His career-high 31 points stole much of the spotlight in the Spartans' 86-76 victory.

GRANT HALVERSON/Associated Press

MORRIS PETERSON SOARS ABOVE THE TAR HEELS' JASON CAPEL FOR A REBOUND.

The Man in the middle

BY JEMELE HILL

Morris Peterson welcomes the burden of being The Man. His mother, Valarie, nicknamed him "Man," and now the rest of the country knows why.

Peterson had the best performance of his career against North Carolina, one that would place him on any All-America list he wasn't on before. He scored a career-high 31 points, leading MSU to an 86-76 win at the Dean Smith Center.

"It ranks up there with the best performances I've seen as both an assistant and a coach," Tom Izzo said.

The Spartans not only notched their most impressive victory of the young season but took some luster out of North Carolina's illustrious history. Michigan State became the first team since South Carolina in the 1928-29 season to defeat the Tar Heels in their home opener.

"I think it will bring our team a little bit closer and make them believe a little bit more," Izzo said.

"We had young guys who had never been in an environment like this," Peterson said. "I thought it was my job to step up and take the initiative."

MORRIS PETERSON DRIVES TO THE BASKET FOR TWO OF HIS GAME-HIGH 31 POINTS.

GRANT HALVERSON/Associated Press

"Michigan State is like a Rolls-Royce without the engine," the nation's No. 1 hoop-aholic, Dick Vitale, said before tip-off. "It just won't be the same without Mateen Cleaves."

But the Spartans got an All-America effort from Peterson. He made amends for his poor performance against Texas in the Puerto Rico Shootout championship game, convincing everyone the Spartans aren't merely in a holding pattern until Cleaves returns from a stress fracture in his right foot.

But more important, they set an example for a school fighting off old insecurities. "They lost their leader, and we've lost ours," Charlie Bell said. "But that doesn't mean you still can't succeed if you want it bad enough.

"We all learn from each other. That's what an athletic program's supposed to be all about. I'm glad we were able to put some smiles back on some Michigan State faces."

"I'm happy that we gave the university and the football team something that everybody can be proud of," Cleaves said. "It's been tough for everybody the last couple days, but these guys showed a lot of toughness and character.

"Man, the way they played tonight, they probably don't have any use for me anymore."

Jayhawks no Kan do in the Great Eight

BELL, A.J. TO THE RESCUE

THE GREAT
EIGHT IN
CHICAGO
PROVIDED
ANOTHER
NATIONAL
STAGE FOR
CHARLIE BELL
AND THE
SPARTANS TO
DRIVE HOME
THEIR STATUS
AS TITLE
CONTENDERS.
BELL SCORED
21 POINTS.

JULIAN H. GONZALEZ

JULIAN H. GONZALEZ

Morris Peterson went up and over the Jayhawks' Andrew Gooden.

BY JEMELE HILL

It's amazing what twisting the hair can do to a jump shot. Charlie Bell always had a jump shot, but the cornrows he sported for the first time against Kansas might have given Bell's jumper a certain pinpoint accuracy not seen this season. Bell scored 21 points as the Spartans defeated No. 5 Kansas, 66-54, in the Great Eight.

"I think it's the braids," Morris Peterson said. "I told Charlie I'm getting some next."

Peterson needed something, as he endured his worst shooting game of the season. He was 3-for-14 from the field, scoring 10 points, but he did collect 10 rebounds for his second double-double of the season.

With Peterson missing his shots, the unlikely duo of Bell and A. J. Granger carried the Spartans. Granger, who outplayed Kansas' 7-foot Eric Chenowith, nearly had a double-double with 13 points and nine rebounds.

"A. J. is probably the best shooter on this team," Bell said. "He missed the first couple of shots, but we just told him to keep shooting. He knocked down some big shots. We have a lot of players on our team who can hurt you in all sorts of ways."

Charlie Bell: Hair apparent

BY DREW SHARP

The look just doesn't fit the fashion motif of the normally conservative Charlie Bell. He fancies himself a throwback, more substance than style. He's high socks and an Afro.

Then Bell showed up at basketball practice with short socks and his hair in cornrows.

"When I saw him come into practice," Tom Izzo said, "I pulled up the collar on my jacket because I thought Latrell Sprewell was in the building."

If Bell keeps playing well, Izzo might even let him clutch the coach's throat. Bell displayed an offensive flair rarely seen since his high school days, when he was the most prolific scorer in Flint prep history.

It's been awhile since Bell carried a team. But his game-high 21 points, efficiency at the point, and customary defensive tenacity were the lift the Spartans needed.

The Bell tolled, and the Spartans rolled.

"Man, if he keeps playing like that," Mateen Cleaves said, "I'll braid his hair for him."

"I'm usually old school, but I just wanted to try something different," Bell said. "It's kind of the new look and it didn't look bad, so I thought I'd keep it for a while. But I couldn't wear the long socks with it. That's old school. And you can't have two schools clashing."

Is an earring or tongue stud next?

"I don't know what I'm going to do," he said. "It all depends on what I feel like."

The Spartans won't care as long as he plays like he did against the Jayhawks.

"It's great because everyone in the country's now getting to see all the things that Charlie can do," Cleaves said. "I guess I've become kind of an unofficial assistant coach. So if I have to grade Charlie as a coach, I'll give him an A-plus. He put us all on his shoulders tonight."

JULIAN H. GONZALEZ

"When I saw him come into practice, I pulled up the collar on my jacket because I thought Latrell Sprewell was in the building."

TOM IZZO

Y2K PROBLEMS

DEC. 11, 1999
ARIZONA 79, MSU 68

"We were outworked, outhustled and outshot"

FREE PRESS STAFF
AND NEWS SERVICES

Mateen Cleaves remained sidelined, and Tom Izzo hinted he would shuffle his starters in the wake of a 79-68 loss at Arizona.

The lineup changes would involve moving point guard David Thomas to the sixth-man spot, starting Charlie Bell at the point, and making freshman Jason Richardson or Mike Chappell a starter.

Against Arizona, Michigan State couldn't contain freshman point guard Jason Gardner, who had a season-high 20 points, nine assists and six rebounds. He played all 40 minutes.

Morris Peterson scored 15 of his 17 points in the second half but was only 5-for-15 from the field. Charlie Bell led the Spartans with 20 points. Michigan State shot 40.3 percent, Arizona 52.9 percent.

"In the past, we've played great defense," Bell said. "But today we didn't play defense at all. I mean, they got dunk after dunk after dunk. When they're shooting a high percentage like they were and we're not shooting that well, it's hard to win."

Tom Izzo didn't like his team's effort. "The last thing I wrote on the chalkboard before we left the locker room at the start of the game was that we needed to get all of the loose balls," Izzo said. "We got none. We were outworked, outhustled and outshot."

DEC. 23, 1999
KENTUCKY 60, MSU 58

Spartans wish they had Cleaves for Christmas

ED REINKE/Associated Press

TOM IZZO WAS ALMOST READY TO THROW IN THE TOWEL AGAINST THE WILDCATS IN LEXINGTON.

BY DREW SHARP

Life without Mateen Cleaves has been an education for Michigan State, a process elevated to another level against Kentucky.

The Spartans were angry. They could have rationalized their 60-58 setback as an understandable road loss without their best pressure player, but they knew they were the better team, and they seethed about letting a game get away from them. And nobody was steamed more than Tom Izzo.

"Can you play guard?" he asked a young man escorting him back to the locker room. "If so, come with me, because I don't have any guards on my team."

Nobody wanted to hear anything about silver linings. "We played scared, and you can quote me on that," Izzo fumed. "I guess we're not the program that some people thought we were, because those teams don't let these opportunities slip away. And if there's anybody in that locker room who's feeling good about themselves because we're still 8-3 after this, then those guys aren't the type of people I want in my program. I don't want people making excuses."

Izzo need not have worried. Each player looked as though Santa had left lumps of coal in his stocking.

"If you want to be successful, you can't rest on your laurels," said Morris Peterson, who scored 18 points but only five in the second half. "Everybody on this team was numb when we got back here because we all knew that this was a game that we lost. I don't know if you could say we panicked, but we did make a lot of bad mistakes."

Michigan State wasted a 26-11 lead, believing the Kiddie 'Cats, as fans call them, would curl up in their litter box.

"Moments like this are what this game's supposed to be all about," Cleaves said. "It's not about being nervous. It's about taking your best shot. If you make it, fine. If you don't, you get back on the bus, shake it off, and go back at it next time."

WHAT ARE THE ODDS?

Maybe Las Vegas knew something Michigan State didn't. The oddsmakers had the Spartans as two-point underdogs to the unranked Wildcats, and things played out between them just as Vegas said they would.

It didn't have to, though. The Spartans lost, 60-58, to Kentucky after squandering a 15-point lead. Last-second shots by Andre Hutson and Morris Peterson bounced off the rim.

DEC. 30, 1999 |
WRIGHT STATE 53, MSU 49

Nothing else could go wrong, Wright?

FREE PRESS NEWS SERVICES

We've got a lot of work to do," Tom Izzo said after the Spartans' 53-49 loss to Wright State at the Nutter Center — known as the Nuthouse — in Dayton, Ohio. "That should fall on my shoulders.

"My team wasn't ready to play," Izzo said. "All that will be remedied in the next week, one way or another."

Wright State scored the first seven points and built a 21-12 lead, and Izzo knew it wasn't going to be easy. "They wanted it more than we did," he said. "They played harder than we did."

Wright State coach Ed Schilling was asked when he first realized that his under-talented team actually had beaten the mighty Spartans.

"When I shook Coach Izzo's hand is when I figured we had them," Schilling said.

ED REINKE/Associated Press

KENTUCKY'S TAYSHAUN PRINCE AND A BAD BOUNCE FOILED ANDRE HUTSON'S LAST-SECOND SHOT.

Cleaves comes back;
Spartans celebrate
in Big Ten opener

HAPPY NEW YEAR

BY JEMELE HILL

At times, Mateen Cleaves looked like what he is — rusty. And at other times he looked like what he can be — the emotional leader of the Spartans.

Cleaves, returning from a stress fracture in his right foot, and the Spartans didn't look their best, but they had enough emotion to propel them to a 76-63 victory over Penn State in a Big Ten opener at the Breslin Center.

Cleaves' numbers weren't much — eight points and five assists in 21 minutes off the bench — but he made a difference.

"He was challenging people defensively," Tom Izzo said. "He made a couple of mistakes. To be off 11 weeks and to do the things he did shows what kind of player he is."

Cleaves brought the energy and his teammates did the rest. Four MSU players scored in double figures. A. J. Granger had 15, Charlie Bell 14, Morris Peterson 12 and Andre Hutson 10. It was a sweet way for the Spartans to begin defending their Big Ten crown.

MSU won its 19th straight conference game, an astounding feat with or without an All-America point guard.

JULIAN H. GONZALEZ

MATEEN CLEAVES CONNECTED ON HIS FIRST SHOT OF THE SEASON.

Should auld acquaintance be forgot ...

BY DREW SHARP

He was back, but it still didn't feel just right.

The first basket off the first jumper, coming just seconds into his first action of the season, was nice. The first blind bullet pass to a teammate for an easy lay-up was sweetly sentimental. But Mateen Cleaves didn't feel completely back until he saw Morris Peterson streaking down the left wing in the second half.

Oh, yes. Here it comes. The season's first Flint air-mail delivery.

The alley-oop brought the crowd out of its seats and returned a sense of normalcy to the Breslin Center. The Spartans were flying again because their captain was back in the cockpit.

"It felt just like old times after that play," said Cleaves, who jumped and danced and pumped his way back down the court afterward, certainly looking like someone whose right foot was completely healed.

"I had been preaching to Morris for the last two months that I couldn't wait until we could hook up again. You have no idea how long I've been waiting for this night."

Eleven weeks exactly.

But he was back. And so, too, were the energy and emotion that rub off on everybody else. Tom Izzo didn't want to play Cleaves more than 20 minutes. But he played him a shade more, and Cleaves scored eight points, dished five assists and received four standing ovations.

When he first checked in at the scorer's table at 16:40 of the first half, the crowd roared. When the official scorer said to him, "Glad to have you back," Cleaves happily clapped his hands like a giddy schoolkid.

And in some ways, he was.

"This was a special evening with the reaction of the crowd and everything," Cleaves said. "I had all this nervous energy, sitting there waiting to get into the game. That's why it felt so good to make that first shot. I wanted to get into the flow as quickly as possible."

"It's a good start," Izzo said. "And now it's time for some guys to re-learn their roles now that he's back."

JULIAN H. GONZALEZ

MATEEN CLEAVES GETS A HELPING HAND FROM MORRIS PETERSON IN HIS FIRST GAME OF THE SEASON. CLEAVES FINISHED WITH EIGHT POINTS AND FIVE ASSISTS.

MOM: I'M FINE, REALLY

Mateen Cleaves' mother, Frances, wasn't completely convinced that her son was fully mended when he told her that he would play against Penn State.

"It took me an hour to finally convince her that I was fine," Cleaves said, "because she knows that I would play even if my foot was still broken. I can't wait to tell her that the foot feels pretty good. I'm fine. I'm healthy. So she can stop worrying."

But isn't that what mothers — and coaches — are for?

21 SKIDDOO: BIG TEN WIN STREAK HALTED

TOM IZZO – FLANKED BY
ASSISTANT COACHES BRIAN
GREGORY (LEFT) AND STAN
HEATH – HAD SEEN
ENOUGH.

JAY LaPRETE/Associated Press

JAN. 20, 2000
OHIO STATE 78, MSU 67

Buckeyes prove they're a worthy challenger

BY JEMELE HILL

The Spartans — who use a 10-man rotation — had plenty of bodies, but against Ohio State not enough of them were ready to shoulder the responsibility of defending the Big Ten championship.

The Spartans fell to their most serious challenger for the conference title, 78-67. Ohio State borrowed a philosophy that MSU implanted last season, when the Spartans capital-ized on Morris Peterson's offensive might as the sixth man. Reserve George Reese scored 19 points for the Buckeyes, who ended a 10-game losing streak to MSU and halted Michigan State's 21-game conference winning streak.

"I told him (OSU coach Jim O'Brien) before the game that his team is getting better because his bench is getting better," Tom Izzo said, "and that really showed when they outscored us, 24-6."

Peterson led MSU with 20 points. But the difference was Reese, whose 11 points in the first half fueled the Buckeyes to a 42-33 halftime lead. The Spartans' reserves — David Thomas, Aloysius Anagonye, Mike Chappell, Jason Richardson and Adam Ballinger — produced zero points and took two shots in the first half.

"I think we have a number of guys who can step up," Peterson said, "but we just need somebody to do it."

"Lucky" Spartans back on track

BY JEMELE HILL

After a 20-point victory and a career-high scoring effort from one of his best players, you would expect the coach to need electrolysis to pull the smile off his face. But not when the coach is MSU's Tom Izzo. Not when defense and rebounding are an issue.

According to Izzo, the Spartans did both poorly in an 82-62 victory over Michigan at Crisler Arena. It was MSU's fourth consecutive victory over U-M and the Spartans' fourth Big Ten win in a row since their 21-game conference streak was snapped by Ohio State.

According to Izzo, the Spartans were lucky to beat Michigan.

Lucky?

Morris Peterson and Mateen Cleaves combined for 51 points, with Peterson scoring a career-high 32 and Cleaves 19. Peterson also grabbed 10 rebounds, and Cleaves added six assists to the best offensive game among the eight he has played since returning from a stress fracture in his right foot.

Andre Hutson had 10 points and 10 rebounds — nine rebounds in the first eight minutes — for his fifth double-double of the season and second in a row. But that didn't appease Izzo.

"If Aloysius Anagonye, A. J. Granger, Adam Ballinger and Andre Hutson don't play better, we're going to get beat by 50," Izzo said. "Print it. Five-oh."

Cleaves responded to Izzo's criticism: "He was kind of disappointed because we didn't play good defense, we didn't dive on the floor for loose balls, and he was right. We played defense at times. You can't play in spurts and go through this conference."

Michigan coach Brian Ellerbe wasn't as stingy with his praise. "We got beat by a great team tonight," he said.

If only this one were for the championship

BY JEMELE HILL

A.J. Granger felt like a crash-test dummy after colliding with Mateen Cleaves early in the second half of Michigan State's victory over Connecticut. So he knew how the Huskies felt when the Spartans were done with them.

MSU trampled Connecticut, 85-66, notching a school-record 24th straight win in the Breslin Center and fifth straight win overall.

"You can't read into it," Tom Izzo cautioned. "That is not the Connecticut team you're going to see next week or the week after that. It was just one of those days."

Izzo, like the Huskies, had to search for an explanation for holding the Huskies to a season-low 17 points in the first half — MSU led by an astounding 29 points at the half —

JAY LaPRETE/Associated Press

FROM LEFT: MATEEN CLEAVES, ANDRE HUTSON, CHARLIE BELL, MAT ISHBIA AND A.J. GRANGER FIRE UP THE RECEIVING LINE FOR JASON RICHARDSON.

and outrebounding the defending national champions, 40-26.

"I was surprised," Cleaves said of MSU's halftime lead, the biggest the Huskies had faced all season. "To win like that? It was unbelievable."

AFTER MSU CLOBBERED THE WOLVERINES, IT WAS SPARTY TIME.

BIG TEN: BIG FINISH

BY MICHAEL ROSENBERG

MARCH 2, 2000
MSU 79, MINNESOTA 43

Spartans hit their stride, have the look of champions

Put away the measuring sticks. When announcers start talking about "REALLY BIG GAMES," pay attention. Morris Peterson said it emphatically: From now on, every game Michigan State plays would be for a championship.

It would start with the regular-season finale, when Michigan State beat Michigan to claim a share of its third straight Big Ten title. "To have three championship rings would be something special," Tom Izzo said.

Four would be even better, especially if the fourth were to be earned on the first Monday night in April. Michigan State had every reason to believe it could win the national championship. The Spartans were built on those twin engines of defense and rebounding, and neither was likely to slump.

When the Spartans hit their out-side shots, as they did in a 79-43 dismantling of Minnesota, no team in the nation is as complete.

"They don't really have a flaw," Minnesota coach Dan Monson said.

The record didn't show it, but these Spartans were better than last year's Final Four team. Izzo even called the first half against Minnesota "pretty." Imagine that. Michigan State, pretty.

This program was built around guys from Flint; around a point guard, Mateen Cleaves, who can't help but commit turnovers; and a bunch of forwards who are told to rebound first and defend second, then concentrate on rebounding and defending.

Pretty?

Izzo was right, though. This was pretty, with Mike Chappell (finally) sinking rainbow three-pointers, Peterson putting a little too much flair in his dunks, and everybody on the team playing unselfishly.

Of course, Izzo — who could find flaws in Michael Jordan if he wore green and white — had no problem coming up with a few for his team.

"You got time?" he said. "There's flaws. At times we don't shoot the ball from the outside. At times our consistency, our defensive aggression, our turnovers have been a problem. We've got enough that I can still earn my money tomorrow and tonight, put it that way."

Perfect? No. The Spartans were not perfect. But they wouldn't have to be.

"It was an incredible day. ... I thought the seniors deserved to have a day — they have done so much for the program, so much for Michigan State. And they earned it." **TOM IZZO**

MARCH 4, 2000 |
MSU 114, MICHIGAN 63

"We weren't rubbing anything in anybody's face," says Cleaves . . . yeah, sure

BY JEMELE HILL

There might not have been words to describe how badly Michigan State beat Michigan in the Big Ten regular-season finale, but there were enough records eclipsed to explain it all.

The Spartans trounced Michigan, 114-63 — the worst pummeling MSU had ever given Michigan and the first time since 1959 that the Spartans scored 100 points against the Wolverines.

With the win, the Spartans

YOU HAD TO HAND IT TO MATEEN CLEAVES AND (FROM LEFT) MORRIS PETERSON, ANDRE HUTSON AND A.J. GRANGER AFTER THEY HANDED THE WOLVERINES A 51-POINT THRASHING IN THE REGULAR-SEASON FINALE.

JULIAN H. GONZALEZ

IT ENDED WITH SMILES ALL AROUND AND A GOOD-BYE KISS AS MATEEN CLEAVES PAID TRIBUTE TO THE BIG BLOCK S AT CENTER COURT OF THE BRESLIN CENTER.

JULIAN H. GONZALEZ

clinched a tie for the Big Ten title, becoming the only team in school history to win or share three straight conference titles.

Since it was senior day, it was only appropriate that a senior had a record-setting individual performance: Mateen Cleaves had 20 assists — a Michigan State and Big Ten single-game record — and eight points. The 20 assists, two short of the NCAA record, moved Cleaves into first place on the Big Ten's all-time assist list with 769.

"It was an incredible day," Tom Izzo said. "I don't think I can downplay it, and I don't think I can change anything. I thought the seniors deserved to have a day — they have done so much for the program, so much for Michigan State. And they earned it."

Standing next to Cleaves' accomplishment was a career-high, 31-point performance by Charlie Bell, who did as much as anyone in the second half to aid Cleaves in reaching the assist record. Bell was 13-of-19 from the field, with four three-pointers.

The Spartans, who set a team record for points in a Big Ten game, sank a school-record 16 three-pointers and ballooned a 27-point halftime lead to as much as 57 points in the second half.

"A win is a win, whether it be by 50 points or by one point," Cleaves said.

"We weren't rubbing anything in anybody's face. We're two class programs. It was one of those special days. Fifty points or one point, we'll take it however it comes."

BIG TEN TOURNAMENT

MORRIS PETERSON (LEFT) AND MATEEN CLEAVES BRING DOWN THE NYLON AT THE UNITED CENTER IN CHICAGO AFTER A SECOND STRAIGHT BIG TEN TOURNAMENT TITLE.

Cleaves: "I'm just happy
to be standing here a winner."

IOWA ALMOST PULLS OFF OPENING-ROUND UPSET

BY JEMELE HILL

It was a bit too predictable for Michigan State: the struggle in the first Big Ten tournament game, building a lead and squandering it, and having a bench that contributes little. Despite it all, MSU managed a 75-65 win over seventh-seeded Iowa at Chicago's United Center.

"Some teams struggle with pulling out the tough games," Mateen Cleaves said. "I'm not satisfied with the way we played, but I am satisfied with the way we grinded it out. I'm just happy to be standing here a winner."

The second-seeded Spartans made it hard on themselves. Four of their starters scored in double figures, but the bench had two shots and four points. And poor play by the reserves during one particular stretch electrified an Iowa team that was just about to wilt.

The Spartans started the game with a 15-4 run. Then the subs came in and the lead diminished. The Hawkeyes outscored the Spartans, 22-10, over the next 11 minutes and took a 26-25 lead at 5:03, Iowa's first lead of the game.

"We had a 15-4 lead, we bring guys in, and we check absolutely nobody," Tom Izzo said. "After that, the game was a dogfight the rest of the way."

And the Iowa player who barked the loudest was junior guard Dean Oliver, who scored a career-high 30 points and almost single-handedly pulled off the upset.

Morris Peterson made some clutch shots in the second half to ensure that the Spartans didn't go down in the first round, as did top-seeded Ohio State. "Toward the end of the game, that was definitely running through my mind," Peterson said.

"The first game is always tough," Cleaves said. "But we made the plays at the end. We found a way to pull it out."

JULIAN H. GONZALEZ

WHEW! RELIEF IS SPELLED OUT ON MATEEN CLEAVES' FACE AS HE GETS A CONGRATULATORY HUG FROM MORRIS PETERSON AFTER MSU HELD OFF THE HAWKEYES.

ANDRE HUTSON HAD NINE POINTS AND FIVE REBOUNDS AGAINST IOWA IN ADDITION TO THIS MIDAIR SNAG OF A LOOSE BALL BETWEEN HAWKEYES DEAN OLIVER (LEFT) AND JASON PRICE.

JULIAN H. GONZALEZ

MORRIS PETERSON REACTS TO HIS THREE-POINTER THAT HELPED BUILD A DOUBLE-DIGIT LEAD IN THE FIRST HALF AGAINST WISCONSIN.

Badgers do everything
but shoot out the lights

ANOTHER CLOSE CALL

BY JEMELE HILL

Wisconsin had fewer turnovers. Wisconsin didn't allow a dunk or an alley-oop. Wisconsin made the Spartans dizzy by sending them through screen after screen after screen. But there was one thing Wisconsin didn't do.

"There are four things we have to do against them, and we generally do three of them well," Badgers coach Dick Bennett said. "We take care of the ball, do a halfway decent job on the glass, and get back on defense. The one thing we seldom do is shoot the ball well enough against them because their defense is that good."

And that's a fairly good explanation for why the Spartans — who pounded out a 55-46 win over Wisconsin — were going to their second straight Big Ten tournament championship game against Illinois.

The Spartans shot 61 percent in the first half; the Badgers were 30.9 percent for the game. "Wisconsin is one of those teams that plays hard the entire 40 minutes," Morris Peterson said. "You have to be ready to check, and you have to be ready to be checked."

Which is why the Spartans thought they were dreaming when they had a 19-point lead at 15:46 of the second half, their largest of the game. But the Badgers went on a 15-2 run and trailed by five with under six minutes to play before MSU put the game out of reach.

"You have to give Wisconsin a lot of credit," Mateen Cleaves said. "They played hard throughout the game, especially in the second half. They made sure we didn't have as many open shots as we did in the first."

JULIAN H. GONZALEZ

MATEEN CLEAVES STARTS A FAST BREAK IN THE SECOND HALF AFTER ONE OF ONLY FOUR BADGERS TURNOVERS.

JULIAN H. GONZALEZ

TOM IZZO WATCHED A 19-POINT LEAD SHRINK TO FIVE.

MARCH 12, 2000
MSU 76
ILLINOIS 61

Spartans win Big Ten tournament
but know their work has just begun

SENIOR CLASS

BY DREW SHARP

Families sometimes bicker. Even brothers go at it once in a while. And often it's the father who must make peace.

Mateen Cleaves and Morris Peterson clashed during a first-half time-out during the Big Ten tournament championship game. But Tom Izzo cooled them off by suggesting that if they didn't shut up, he'd have freshman behemoth Aloysius Anagonye silence them.

Cleaves and Peterson cracked up, and it was back to business, back to focusing on the bigger picture. And then it was all about getting to the mountaintop, the ultimate destination that eluded Michigan State in 1999.

MSU's second straight conference tournament title — a 76-61 victory over Illinois — was old stuff for most of the Spartans. They had grown accustomed to No. 1 NCAA tournament seeds, championship caps and T-shirts. It was no big deal to the veterans such as Cleaves, Peterson and Andre Hutson.

However, Jason Richardson, a freshman, was caught up in the moment and began joyously hugging teammates. But when he got to Hutson, he was met with an intimidating, emotionless stare. The look told the youngster this wasn't the goal, merely the first step.

Nothing short of the national championship would do, because these Spartans were special.

"I'll tell you this," Izzo said. "How long we stay in the tournament won't be a factor in how proud I am of what this team has done, especially this senior class. I'm not going to be able to relish the remaining time that I have with these guys, but I hope people watching will.

"They're so special, and we should savor them because we may not see the likes of a senior class like this again."

JULIAN H. GONZALEZ

THE CELEBRATION WAS ON FOR MORRIS PETERSON AND THE SPARTANS AFTER A FINAL, FRUSTRATING TURNOVER FOR ILLINOIS AND SERGIO MCCLAIN.

Savor them, because the senior class of Cleaves, Peterson and A. J. Granger belong to the first 100-win class in MSU history. Savor them, because Cleaves and Peterson were an anomaly in today's get-me-to-the-NBA-as-quickly-as-possible world of college basketball. They were potential first-round draft choices in 1999 but stayed in school, bound by one common goal — tearing down the only nets that really matter, the ones from the last game.

JULIAN H. GONZALEZ

Charlie Bell takes it to the hoop against Illinois' Brian Cook and Sergio McClain.

JULIAN H. GONZALEZ

"When I was younger," Cleaves said, "I always dreamed about being in the Final Four or the championship game, the clock running down and you're down by a point. You always dream about making the big shot and winning the game and having everybody going crazy around you. That's why you play the game. The money's fine, but you play because you like winning."

When Peterson heard his name announced as the MVP of the Big Ten tournament, the first congratulatory hug came from Cleaves. It was easy to read Peterson's lips. "I love you," he told Cleaves, his teammate, his brother.

JULIAN H. GONZALEZ

NOTHING BUT NET: MORRIS PETERSON AND MATEEN CLEAVES ARE ON TOP OF THE WORLD AFTER WINNING THE BIG TEN TOURNEY. AT LEFT: THE SPARTANS HAVE THE LAST LAUGH AGAINST ILLINOIS.

A CHAMPIONSHIP WITHIN THEIR GRASP, THE SPARTANS JOINED HANDS ACROSS THE MIDWEST — FROM CLEVELAND TO AUBURN HILLS TO INDIANAPOLIS — TO REACH THE APEX OF NCAA BASKETBALL GLORY.

MARCH 16, 2000
MSU 65
VALPARAISO 38

Starters, subs
step on some toes
in Big Dance opener

SPARTY HEARTY VS. VALPO

BY MITCH ALBOM

This is when you know you're for real in college basketball. When you use the first game of the NCAA tournament to get your subs some playing time.

That's pretty much what Tom Izzo did on the first rung of the ladder of dreams. While most teams in the Big Dance treat every game as a sprint — All-out, men! No letup! Do or die! Now is the time! — the Spartans, luxuriously, can view it as a marathon. Take it slow. Be smart. Work on what you'll need for later.

After all, let's be honest, Michigan State didn't really need to worry about losing to Valparaiso, its 16th-seeded opponent. A bigger challenge would be spelling the name of the school.

Check that: A bigger challenge would be spelling the names of the Valpo players. This was a roster that boasted two players from Croatia, one from the Czech Republic, one from Latvia and one from Finland. No offense, but when you say "big dance" to those guys, they're thinking Independence Day.

Anyhow, Izzo knew Valpo would be Alpo, even if he wouldn't admit it. "You're always worried about a first-round upset," he said after the Spartans, uh, eked out a 65-38 victory. "They're a good team. They can

JULIAN H. GONZALEZ

AS EASY AS 1-2-3: MORRIS PETERSON TURNED THIS LAY-UP INTO A THREE-POINT PLAY.

MSU HELD VALPO TO 25 PERCENT SHOOTING, GOOD FOR A SMILE ANYTIME FROM TOM IZZO AND HIS PLAYERS.

ALOYSIUS ANAGONYE (LEFT) AND ADAM BALLINGER SANDWICH VALPO'S IVAN VUJIC, WHO MISSES THIS SECOND-HALF SHOT.

do some things."

True. But a cocker spaniel can do some things, too. If Valpo were that good, why did the Crusaders shoot 25 percent for the night? Why did they need nearly the whole game to break 30 points? If they were so good, why did they call time-out after 44 seconds?

I'm not kidding here. Two quick baskets by the Spartans and — tweeeet! — the Valpers were on the sideline, huddling up.

COACH: Are we in the right place?

PLAYERS: Rztyazca a ytaer? (Serbo-Croatian for "Why are you asking us?")

Anyhow, Izzo, a smart guy, could see this developing. Which is why, within the first four minutes, he already had inserted freshmen Jason Richardson and Adam Ballinger. A few moments later, here came backups Mike Chappell and David Thomas. So much for the starting lineup. Ballinger had six points before Mateen Cleaves had any. Richardson

JULIAN H. GONZALEZ

HAVE SPIRIT, WILL TRAVEL: AWAY FROM BRESLIN COMFORTS, FANS CREATE A TEMPORARY IZZONE IN CLEVELAND.

was the leading scorer at half-time.

Subs and starters switched partners on the fly, like a hardwood square dance. Not that it made any difference to Team Benetton, a.k.a. The Valpo Crusaders, who had only three points — three points? — until 6:45 was left in the first half.

"Were they speaking English out there?" someone asked Ballinger. "Yeah," he said, "but with an accent."

By the time the game ended,

it was an equal-opportunity night for MSU. Backup Ballinger logged nearly as many minutes (20) as starter Andre Hutson (21). Chappell had nearly as many minutes (14) as starter Charlie Bell (16). And Richardson, the slithering freshman, had nearly as many minutes (25) as All-America and Big Ten player of the year Morris Peterson (27).

This, of course, was smart basketball by Izzo and his staff. The knock on this team is its

bench and its depth, so why not work on those soft spots? Being able to do it under tournament conditions is even better, like getting to test your parachutes during combat with no fear of being shot down.

Anyhow, one-sixth of the climb to glory was over. A dangerous step, for sure, because bigger favorites than the Spartans have fallen in the first round. Not that I can think of any right now, but it seems like the proper thing to say.

OPPOSITE: IN PRACTICE, WARM-UPS AND GAMES, JASON RICHARDSON GAVE FANS A TANTALIZING GLIMPSE OF THE SPARTANS' FUTURE.

Utah backs MSU into first-half corner

GUT-CHECK TIME FOR SPARTANS

JULIAN H. GONZALEZ

MSU SHOWS THE UNITED FRONT IT WOULD NEED TO THWART UTAH'S UPSET BID.

BY JEMELE HILL

What Tom Izzo said at halftime couldn't be printed in a family newspaper. What happened 20 minutes after that could: Michigan State 73, Utah 61.

In the throes of survive-and-advance, the final tally is all that matters, and the Spartans advanced to the Sweet 16 for the third consecutive year.

"These guys had a character check at halftime," Izzo said. "And these three seniors (Mateen Cleaves, A. J. Granger and Morris Peterson) answered the bell like they have for four years. I'm just pleased to get out of here with a win."

Cleaves rose to a level known only to All-Americas, scoring 21 points and dishing five assists, with 13 of his points coming at crucial moments in the second half. Cleaves was 4-for-7 on his three-point tries, a season best, and tied a season high with seven field goals. He was 7-for-14 from the floor.

Andre Hutson was two points shy of his

JULIAN H. GONZALEZ

ANDRE HUTSON WAS IN THE MIDDLE OF THINGS MOST OF THE NIGHT, WITH 19 POINTS AND EIGHT REBOUNDS.

career best, tying his season high with 19 points and adding eight rebounds, and proving to be a worthwhile adversary to Utah big man Hanno Mottola.

You can't blame Utah coach Rick Majerus for his game plan: Cover the daylights out of Morris Peterson, then make Cleaves — whose outside shooting is sometimes suspect — beat you. The plan worked for a half; Utah led, 35-32.

Then Cleaves led the comeback. He threaded a pass to Hutson at 17:24 for two points. Cleaves then scored MSU's next five points on a three-pointer and lay-up, giving the Spartans their first lead since early in the first half.

"Cleaves stung us tonight," Majerus said. "We picked our poison and wanted Cleaves to shoot the ball, and he did, and he beat us."

HAVE YOU CHEST-
BUMPED A
FLINTSTONE
TODAY? ANDRE
HUTSON AND
MATEEN CLEAVES
DEMONSTRATE THE
PROPER TECHNIQUE
FOR ADDING
EMPHASIS TO A
GOOD PLAY.

JULIAN H. GONZALEZ

Backs to the wall ... Cleaves to the rescue

JULIAN H. GONZALEZ

"Mateen's been vocal before,
but there was a demon inside of him today."
MORRIS PETERSON

BY DREW SHARP

Mateen Cleaves had seen enough.

He wasn't ready for his collegiate curtain call, so he got in the faces of his buddies from Flint during an impassioned halftime diatribe, challenging the toughness of Morris Peterson and Charlie Bell.

He nearly got into Peterson's uniform in the second half, grabbing him by the seat of his shorts, pulling him chest-to-chest, imploring Peterson to step up or step out.

"Mateen's been vocal before," Peterson said, "but there was a demon inside of him today."

A national championship demon.

Cleaves saw everything Michigan State had worked for slipping away. And as he has done so often during his four years at Michigan State, he pushed his teammates to victory.

In the second half against undermanned Utah, Cleaves made the three-pointer when he had to. Got the steal when he needed it. Fed the ball inside to Andre Hutson when the opportunity was there. And kicked some tail when necessary.

"For whatever reason, we just didn't play with any emotion early," Cleaves said. "So I made a point to a couple of guys who I thought weren't playing as hard as they should have."

"Without Mateen, we're probably going home very disappointed over the opportunity we would've missed," Tom Izzo said. "He grabbed us by the you-know-what and told us to follow him. That's been typical of his time here. I've always said that he might be the best leader we've ever had here at Michigan State, including Magic (Earvin Johnson). And you saw what the will to win is all about in his performance out there."

MARCH 23, 2000
MSU 75
SYRACUSE 58

Spartans sputter in the first half, then take charge

GREEN MEANS GO — ORANGEMEN SEE RED

JULIAN H. GONZALEZ

GETTING DOWN TO BUSINESS: TOM IZZO JETTISONED HIS SUIT COAT FOR THE FIRST TIME ALL SEASON IN THE SECOND HALF.

BY MITCH ALBOM

Time after time, their best hope went into the belly of the beast. Time after time, he came away bloody. Here was Mateen Cleaves, the heart of the Spartans, driving into the Syracuse defense, twisting, leaping, rolling up a shot and — swat! Rejected.

Another drive, a fast break this time, surely now he's going to score — swat! Blocked again, into the hands of a Syracuse player, into the hands of another Syracuse player, into the hands of another Syracuse player who jammed it home for a big lead.

Michigan State was a balloon losing air. Cleaves missed every shot he tried, inside and outside. His checks were being cashed by the Orangemen, and when the halftime horn sounded, he walked off the court with nothing, no points, no rebounds, no lead.

And his teammates, so used to looking to him for leadership, had little more to show for themselves. Morris Peterson had one basket in the first 10 seconds and was silent the rest of the half. A. J. Granger seemed to be dancing on hot coals, awkward in his shot, tentative with his rebounds. The bench had a total of two free throws.

Let's face it: The Spartans were getting smoked at the Palace — on a court so close to home, it was painted green.

If ever there was a time to panic, a time to figure this whole MSU hysteria was more dream than reality, it was now, this halftime, as the Spartans trailed red-hot Syracuse — a team that started the season with 19 straight victories — by a fat 10 points, right?

Not so fast. Remember this: The young do not judge time well. Freshmen think there is an endless supply of it, sophomores worry prematurely about it running out. But seniors? This is where they are invaluable.

A senior has weathered the storms. A senior knows a midterm is not a final, one beer is not the same as six beers — and a basketball game is 40 minutes, not 20.

"If this was gonna be our last 20 minutes," Peterson, the senior, would later say, "we were gonna make sure it was a game."

"At halftime, I yelled the worst things I've said to my teammates all year," Cleaves, another senior, would add. "But we were not gonna take off these jerseys without a fight."

Hmm. Second half, anyone?

Or should I say second act? By the time this game was over, you couldn't connect the second half to the first if you had 100 feet of cable. If the first half was the Spartans' flailing in the deep end of a pool, the second half was MSU on the roof with a garden hose, laughing, untouchable, raining down three-pointers on Syracuse in

MATEEN CLEAVES' LAY-UP BETWEEN ORANGEMEN JASON HART AND PRESTON SHUMPERT HELPED CAP A GAME-CLOSING 22-2 RUN.

a soaking display of tenacity.

First Granger — another senior — swished a three-pointer, cutting the lead. Then Cleaves nailed a three-pointer, whittling it some more. Peterson answered with a three-pointer. Cleaves echoed with another. Peterson hit another.

The Spartans hit six three-pointers in nine consecutive attempts in six minutes. And in the next six minutes, they had two more treys and three lay-ups. In the final six minutes, Charlie Bell had nine points, three rebounds, a steal and an assist — all by himself.

The Spartans would shoot 68 percent for the second half, which means two out of every three shots they took went through.

"Was it fear that brought out that performance?" someone asked Cleaves after the Spartans more than doubled the Orangemen in the second half, outscoring them, 51-24, to finish with an eye-rubbing, 75-58 victory and a berth in the Elite Eight.

"It wasn't fear," Cleaves said. "It was a sense of urgency. You know, you're thinking it could be your last game. I mean, I don't wanna say it was fear." He shrugged. "Well, OK. It was fear."

So what did the Spartans learn?

"We need to get better starts in our next games," Cleaves said,

Saved by the Bell

BY HELENE ST. JAMES

With visions of a championship fading fast, Tom Izzo knew the time had come to prod one of his stars to shoot a little higher. The way Charlie Bell was playing wasn't going to get the Spartans anywhere but home.

Early in the second half against Syracuse, Izzo approached Bell, leaned over and snapped, "You ready to play yet?"

"That's Izzo," Bell said afterward, wearing an ice pack on his tendinitis-prone left knee. "I wasn't playing well on defense, and I wasn't being aggressive on offense, and that's one of the things he does to motivate you — he gets in your face.

"I was passive in the first half. My confidence was never gone, I just wasn't looking for my shot, and I wasn't being aggressive. I started to look for my shot a little more — be aggressive and not hesitate on it."

Bell recovered from a three-point, two-turnover first half with nine points in the second. He had four assists and only two turnovers in 29 minutes.

"Charlie came alive," Mateen Cleaves said.

CHARLIE BELL SCORED NINE OF HIS 12 POINTS DURING THE SECOND-HALF BLITZ THAT SQUEEZED THE ORANGE.

JULIAN H. GONZALEZ

MORRIS PETERSON RECEIVES AN EXCITED HUG FROM ANDRE HUTSON AFTER PETERSON HIT A THREE-POINTER THAT GAVE MSU A 63-58 LEAD WITH 4:42 LEFT.

JULIAN H. GONZALEZ

JULIAN H. GONZALEZ

THREE DOWN, THREE TO GO: IT'S A TRIANGLE OF RELIEF AS MORRIS PETERSON, TOM IZZO AND MATEEN CLEAVES CELEBRATE THE FRUITS OF THEIR LABORS.

smiling. "I'm tired of giving these halftime speeches."

You think he was tired? To his left sat Tom Izzo, who looked as if he'd melted off about 10 pounds. By the second half, Izzo had removed his sports jacket and rolled up the sleeves of his white shirt. He was a foreman ready to start the presses.

But when it was over, he met two of his senior stars at center court, Peterson (21 points) and Cleaves (10 points, seven assists), and he laughed with them and hugged them, and they seemed to be sharing a secret confidence. They had stared the devil in the face, and they were still here.

"HEY, I LIKE A CHAL-LENGE!" Izzo yelled to a friend.

More to the point, his players could handle one. That's enough to make any coach smile. And enough to give any college team an edge on a championship. Especially players who know that 20 minutes is not 40 minutes, one game is not six games, and the final buzzer sounds different than all the buzzers that come before it.

MARCH 25, 2000
MSU 75
IOWA STATE 64

Hutson holds the fort until help arrives

SPARTANS STRIKE LIKE A CYCLONE

DAVID P. GILKEY (opposite); JULIAN H. GONZALEZ

ANDRE HUTSON ROSE TO THE OCCASION AGAINST ALL-AMERICA MARCUS FIZER OF IOWA STATE, OUTSCORING FIZER, 17-15.

OPPOSITE: FEEL THE POWER! MORRIS PETERSON SLAMS THE DOOR ON IOWA STATE.

BY MICK McCABE

Andre Hutson, MSU's defensive-minded center, proved he can play both ends of the court in the Spartans' 75-64 victory over Iowa State in the Midwest Regional final at the Palace.

Before the tournament, Hutson and Tom Izzo had a little chat. "Coach Izzo brought me in and told me he felt we couldn't play for a national championship without an inside presence," Hutson said.

Now the Spartans were two victories from their first NCAA title in 21 seasons, and Hutson had become an incredible inside presence — a scoring option to go along with the excellent defense he had played all season.

Against Iowa State, he was matched against Marcus Fizer, the Cyclones' powerful 6-8, 265-pound All-America, whom many consider the top player in the country. Hutson held Fizer to 15 points, eight below his season average, on 6-for-15 shooting.

But Hutson did more than play excellent defense. He contributed 17 points on 6-for-9 shooting. He also outrebounded Fizer, 11-4.

"He's pretty much the best player I've ever faced," Hutson said. "He's big and strong and knows how to score. He's got a lot of moves. But we decided to take it to him. He's a great offensive player, but I could tell on film that he's not a great shot blocker on defense. So we decided to go

NCAA TOURNAMENT   **51**

right at him."

MSU's strategy to attack Fizer became evident early in the second half. Hutson scored consecutive baskets, giving MSU a 40-36 lead. After Iowa State scored 12 straight, taking the lead, 48-40, Hutson responded with a pair of free throws and a three-point play, putting MSU back in the game.

Then, for the second time in the regional, the Spartans wiped out their opponent's lead with a blurring rally. The Spartans needed just two minutes to turn a 61-55 deficit into a 64-61 lead before finishing off the Cyclones with an 11-3 run. In the final six minutes against Syracuse, the Spartans squeezed off the final 17 points to barrel past the Orangemen.

"Coach always says tough players win," said Morris Peterson, who scored all but five of his 18 points in the second half against Iowa State. "And I thought down the stretch, we showed how tough we were."

A. J. Granger also scored 18 points for the Spartans, the last No. 1 seed left in the tournament.

Hutson made Fizer work on both ends of the floor, not permitting him to rest when his team didn't have the ball. Once Fizer touched the ball on offense, the Spartans, led by Hutson, surrounded him.

"I liked the way he battled Fizer all night," Izzo said. "He really went after him. I thought he rebounded so well. He really came up with some big rebounds."

During an interview session the day before Iowa State and MSU were to meet, Fizer was asked for his impressions of Hutson. "I don't know anything about Andre Hutson," Fizer said.

After the game, a small smile crept across Hutson's face in the steamy MSU locker room when the story was relayed to him. "I'm pretty sure he knows something about me now," Hutson said.

JULIAN H. GONZALEZ

THE PALACE DANCE FLOOR WAS ALL GREEN. NEXT STOP: INDIANAPOLIS.

ERIC SEALS

TALK THE TALK: FROM LEFT, MORRIS PETERSON, A. J. GRANGER AND MATEEN CLEAVES HAVE YET ANOTHER HAPPY TALE TO TELL.

"Somebody was guiding those shots in"

ERIC SEALS

JOY MIXED WITH SADNESS: MORRIS PETERSON'S MOM, VALARIE, SHARES A HUG DURING THE PALACE CELEBRATION.

BY JEMELE HILL

Morris Peterson climbed high on the ladder, snipping a piece of the net that symbolized Michigan State's return to the Final Four. During the celebration, Peterson's words ran together as he talked to reporters because he was so excited, riding the emotion of a 75-64 victory over Iowa State.

Minutes later, while wearing a Final Four cap and T-shirt, the best moment in Peterson's life collided with his worst. In MSU's locker room at the Palace — in the company of his father and mother, Tom Izzo and teammate and roommate Mateen Cleaves — Peterson was told that his grandmother had died the morning of the game.

Clara Mae Spencer was 72. She had suffered a stroke in February and died from complications.

Peterson went from being the Midwest Regional's Most Outstanding Player for the second straight season to a grieving grandson in a matter of minutes.

"My grandmother was like my best friend," Peterson said. "She'd do anything for me. It was hard for me. I was so close to her. After the season, I was planning to go see her."

Peterson's grandmother was a big part of his childhood. As a toddler, he stayed with her frequently in Mississippi. She let Peterson beat her at video games because he couldn't beat his mother or two sisters. She let Peterson beat her at basketball, too, because he couldn't beat anyone else.

Peterson's family didn't tell him about his grandmother's death until after the game. "She was a big fan of his," said Valarie Peterson, Morris' mother. "She would not have wanted him to be unhappy."

But even though he didn't know, Peterson said he had a persistent feeling during the game that someone was watching over him. When Peterson soared high for an alley-oop dunk with 2:04 to play, he said he felt it. When he sank a three-pointer minutes before the crucial dunk, he said he felt it.

Peterson scored 13 of his 18 points in the second half. "My grandmother was right there with me," Peterson said. "It seemed like somebody was guiding those shots in. I didn't know she passed away, but I really felt her."

Grandmother's memory puts
a charge in MoPete's game

'I KNEW SHE WAS WATCHING ME'

BY DREW SHARP

One game. One win. One dream. A season-long mission reduced to its simplest form.

"It's hard to imagine that we're just one away from achieving something that you've dreamed about ever since you were a little kid," Morris Peterson said after Michigan State's 53-41 national semifinal victory over Wisconsin. "It always seemed so far away, but it's so close now that you can practically taste it."

The dream began following the 1999 national semifinal. The Spartans fell to Duke in a game few believed the Spartans could win. But it was in those moments following the defeat that the resolve was forged that drove the 1999-2000 Spartans.

It was then that Mateen Cleaves knew he was returning for his senior season. The NBA could wait. And it was then that Peterson made up his mind that if he were fortunate enough to get another chance at a Final Four, he would play more aggressively.

"I knew Pete was going to have a great game after I saw him sky for that offensive rebound off the first shot of the game," Cleaves said. "He just soared for the ball. I knew he was charged up then. His intensity was up, and he was going to give us the emotion we needed."

Peterson credited his late grandmother's spirit for providing the jolt. For a change, it was Peterson who

DAVID P. GILKEY

MORRIS PETERSON, WHO BAGGED THE BADGERS WITH 16 SECOND-HALF POINTS, DEDICATED THE VICTORY TO HIS LATE GRANDMOTHER.

IT WASN'T PRETTY, BUT IT WAS EFFECTIVE. A.J. GRANGER (NO. 43), MORRIS PETERSON AND COMPANY PUT THE SQUEEZE ON THE BADGERS, HOLDING THEM TO 17 POINTS IN THE FIRST HALF.

DAVID P. GILKEY

awakened his slumbering teammates with a blistering second half against Wisconsin, scoring 16 of his game-high 20 points in the final 20 minutes. He also snared seven rebounds for the game.

"It's been a difficult last couple of days for me," Peterson said. "I think that's why I was so fired up. But my teammates have been great. They just told me to go out and play hard. It's been an emotional time, but I was determined to be as aggressive as I could."

Peterson attended his grandmother's funeral in Mississippi two days before the semifinal game. During the game, he often pointed toward the heavens after making a basket to salute her.

"Yeah, I pointed to her just to let her know that I knew she was watching me," he said. "She's always going to be with me, and I wanted to make that extra effort to let her know that I feel her presence."

Peterson had been reminded of

Tom Izzo confers with the man of the moment. Peterson finished with 20 points.

life's cruelties in the week leading up to the Final Four. There are no guarantees in either life or basketball, and you must take advantage of the special opportunities when they present themselves. He believed the best way to honor his grandmother was to win the national championship that she heard him talk about for much of his life.

"I wanted the ball," Peterson said.

"Just like Mateen was saying last week in the Iowa State game and the Syracuse game. I needed to be more aggressive and take charge of the situation. I was getting open, and I felt like I could make something happen."

No one expected a classic when MSU and Wisconsin met for the fourth time this season, but MSU's victory achieved a new low in entertainment. The Spartans didn't score

a field goal for the final 12 minutes of the first half. The Badgers had some multiple-minute scoring droughts themselves.

"We knew that this was going to be a battle because that's the way Wisconsin plays," Tom Izzo said. "I'm sure it wasn't a pretty game to watch, but that's the point — it doesn't matter how nice they look. All that matters is winning."

MATEEN CLEAVES, HELD TO 11 POINTS, SAID MORRIS PETERSON GAVE THE SPARTANS "THE EMOTION WE NEEDED."

Gators try it all,
but nothing can stop the Spartans

ALL STATE!

BY JEMELE HILL

Florida tried just about everything to keep the ball out of Mateen Cleaves' hands.

The Gators tried the press. Didn't work. Cleaves battered them with lay-ups. They tried trapping him at the top of the key. Didn't work. Cleaves got the ball anyway, sinking jumpers and three-pointers.

Then with 16:18 left and the Spartans staring the national championship right between the eyes, Cleaves suffered a sprained right ankle after tangling with Florida guard Teddy Dupay.

But they couldn't keep him out then, either.

Behind Cleaves' will and grit, the Spartans won the national championship with an 89-76 victory at the RCA Dome in Indianapolis. It was their second national title, coming 21 years after Magic Johnson led them to their first.

Cleaves finished with 18 points, four assists and the tournament's Most Outstanding Player award.

"That guy has the heart of a lion," Tom Izzo said.

The Gators had youth, depth and brashness, but they were no match for MSU's experience and senior leadership. All three seniors played key roles.

Morris Peterson scored 21 points, keeping the Gators at bay with deadly three-point shooting. Fifteen of his points came in the second half.

And MSU's third senior, A. J. Granger, hit key three-pointers and finished with a team-high nine rebounds.

Michigan State shot 55.9 percent from the field, including 11-for-22 from three-point range.

Cleaves was having a fine game before the injury. He scored 13 first-half points. But when he left, Florida had cut the Spartans' lead to 50-44.

The injury happened when Cleaves shot past the Florida press, seemingly headed for a lay-up. Dupay followed closely. He and Cleaves fought for position. Dupay shoved Cleaves and was whistled for a foul. Cleaves went up with a shot and landed hard on his right ankle, writhing in pain for a few minutes on the floor. Hunched on his knees, he screamed: "It's broke! I know it's broke!"

It wasn't. Cleaves limped to the

JULIAN H. GONZALEZ

MORRIS PETERSON
WAS A CLASS ACT,
SCORING 15
SECOND-HALF
POINTS AGAINST
FLORIDA. "I GUESS
THIS IS THE PERFECT
ENDING," HE SAID.

NCAA TOURNAMENT   **59**

MATEEN CLEAVES LED THE CHARGE, SCORING 18 POINTS ON 7-FOR-11 SHOOTING, UNTIL AN ANKLE INJURY KNOCKED HIM DOWN BUT NOT OUT.

ERIC SEALS

locker room and returned less than five minutes later.

"I was definitely going to try to come back," Cleaves said. "I told the trainer that they were going to have to amputate my leg to keep me out of this one."

Peterson, who scored six points in the first half, seized the mantle and shot 5-for-7 from the field in the second half. Granger scored 10 points in the half and tied his career high of 19 points for the game.

Charlie Bell ran the offense in Cleaves' absence, scoring nine points, with five assists and eight rebounds.

The bench that was disappointing all season came to life, too. Reserve Mike Chappell finished with five points, all coming on MSU's first two post-Cleaves possessions. He hit a three, then scored on a put-back, giving MSU a 55-44 lead.

"We weren't going to back down when we lost Mateen," Chappell said. "There was no way we were going to let this one slip away."

Backup forward Jason Richardson took advantage of the game's fast pace, scoring nine points.

"Oh my God," Cleaves said after the game. "This is what I came back for. It was a total group effort."

JULIAN H. GONZALEZ

Down low or from three-point range, it didn't matter, A.J. Granger was a constant thorn in the Gators' side, finishing with 19 points.

When Cleaves returned at 11:51, he was hobbling, but his heart didn't weaken. He couldn't penetrate, couldn't run, but his presence was enough. He didn't score another point, but he didn't need to.

The Spartans rebounded and defended better than they had all game. Forward Mike Miller, the Gators' leading scorer, was held to 10 points on 2-for-5 shooting. Florida's starting guard combination of Dupay and Justin Hamilton produced zero points and one assist. Florida shot 43.3 percent, 33.3 from three-point range.

Center Udonis Haslem led the Gators with a game-high 27 points.

"It's not like this is Mateen Cleaves and a bunch of nobodies," Miller said. "They're a great basketball team."

The Spartans led by as many as 20 points.

"I take my hat off to my seniors," Izzo said. "They came in four years ago and we made some promises. Now we answered those promises."

ERIC SEALS

MATEEN CLEAVES SHOT PAST THE FLORIDA PRESS WITH TEDDY DUPAY IN PURSUIT. CLEAVES WENT UP WITH A SHOT, THE PAIR TANGLED AND CLEAVES LANDED HARD ON HIS RIGHT ANKLE.

He waited a lifetime,
and it was worth it ...

MATEEN'S SHINING MOMENT

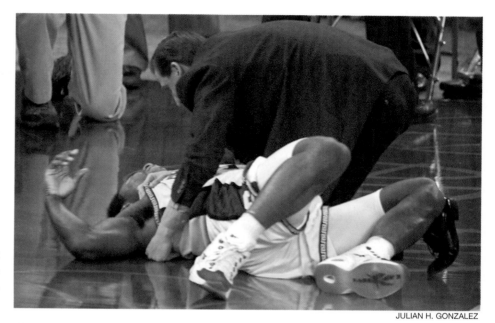

JULIAN H. GONZALEZ

CLEAVES WRITHED IN PAIN, CALLING OUT: "IT'S BROKE! I KNOW IT'S BROKE!"

For five frightening minutes, it looked like Michigan State would have to end the season the way it began — without its leader.

The Spartans saw the tears in Mateen Cleaves' eyes and the anguish on his face as he writhed on the floor after his right ankle rolled underneath him. Tom Izzo leaned over him, trying to console him, but deep down fearing the worst.

"It's broke!" Cleaves yelled. "I know it's broke!"

The dream couldn't die this way.

This was Cleaves' moment. The reason he put the NBA on hold for a year. And until the injury, the national-title game against Florida was his show.

But the toughness of a town and its basketball heritage was there for a national TV audience to see as Cleaves returned in a scene reminiscent of Willis Reed hobbling from the locker room to lead the New York Knicks to victory in Game 7 of the 1970 NBA Finals.

Cleaves put the "stone" in Flint.

"I told the trainer that they were going to have to amputate my leg to keep me out of this one," Cleaves said. "I went back to the locker room and shed a few tears. But I told myself, 'Not now.' I wanted to get back in there. I wanted to win this game."

Adversity had molded this team since two weeks before the season, when doctors inserted screws in Cleaves' right foot to repair a stress fracture. Five months later, the Spartans were champions of college basketball after an 89-76 victory over Florida.

"This doesn't get any more storybook for Mateen," a teary-eyed Izzo said. "He not only comes back for a senior year. He comes back from an injury. And then to have everything seem to turn on him like it did when he went down tonight, only to come back. I don't know if I'm more emotional right now for myself or for him."

Much happier tears streamed down Cleaves' cheeks when he was surrounded by the three things that moved and motivated him more than anything else — his mother, Frances, his father, Herbert, and the NCAA championship trophy. The three of them swung with the rhythm as "One Shining Moment" — Cleaves' personal anthem for as long as he has played college ball — was played with a video on the RCA Dome's screens.

Afterward he buried his head, softly sobbing on his mother's shoulder.

JULIAN H. GONZALEZ

Tom Izzo tended to his fallen leader. "But once I saw it wasn't broken, I told Mateen, 'OK, you have a few minutes to get it taped and then get back out here.'" Izzo said.

> "I told the trainer that they were going to have
> to amputate my leg to keep me out of this one."
> **MATEEN CLEAVES**

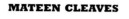

ERIC SEALS

CLEAVES GOT UP GINGERLY, LIMPED TO THE LOCKER ROOM AND RETURNED TO THE GAME LESS THAN FIVE MINUTES LATER.

"Oh God, this is just the greatest feeling you can think of," Cleaves said. "This has been the goal ever since last year when we walked off the floor after losing to Duke. We said we were coming back here and we were going to win it. And we did it! We did it!"

"We" is certainly the appropriate word here. The Spartans didn't fold when they lost their captain. When Izzo told the team that Cleaves' ankle might be broken, Morris Peterson looked to everyone and said, "Then let's just get it done for him."

When Cleaves returned less than five minutes after he left, Florida had to know it was done. The Gators knocked him down, but they couldn't knock him out. He won the tournament's Most Outstanding Player award, and it could have been as much for his courage and composure.

"That's why he's the leader," Peterson said. "I knew he was coming back even when they were saying he had broke it. Nothing was going to keep him out of this. This just meant too much to him."

You'd think that Cleaves was beyond proving himself after 103 career victories, three straight Big Ten regular-season championships, two consecutive conference tournament titles, two straight Final Fours, and one national championship game.

You'd think that a battle-tested senior, possessing the mettle made for these moments, was beyond answering to a legion of doubters following a sloppy semifinal effort against Wisconsin. And when he drilled his first three-pointer midway through the first half, he wagged his

Just like old times

ERIC SEALS

GREEN GIANTS — EARVIN JOHNSON AND MATEEN CLEAVES — SHARE A MAGIC MOMENT AFTER THE CHAMPIONSHIP GAME.

BY MICK MCCABE

Earvin Johnson was having a flashback. It was 1979 again and his Spartans were playing Ohio State. The Buckeyes were 8-0 in the Big Ten. The Spartans were 4-4, and only the Big Ten champion was guaranteed a spot in the NCAA tournament.

Johnson sprained an ankle in the second half and hobbled off the court. He came back to a thunderous ovation that shook Jenison Field House and led MSU to an 84-79 victory in overtime that propelled the Spartans to a 10-game winning streak and the NCAA championship.

Early in the second half against Florida, Mateen Cleaves sustained a sprained right ankle and was helped to the locker room. Like Johnson, Cleaves returned.

"Oh yeah, I was thinking about that game," Johnson said after MSU's national championship victory. "But I knew Mateen was coming back.

"This is why he came back. Mateen needed this more than he needed the NBA. He needed this championship. Now, no matter whatever happens to him for the rest of his life, he will be known as a champion."

> "This doesn't get any more storybook for Mateen. ... I don't know if I'm more emotional right now for myself or for him."
> **TOM IZZO**

tongue as if to say, "Take that!"

Until the final, Florida had held opposing point guards to a seven-point average and 27 percent shooting through the tournament. Cleaves scored 18 points and shot 7-for-11 from the floor.

Any more questions?

"But I've been hearing that stuff so much throughout my career that it doesn't matter anymore," Cleaves said. "People are going to keep talking about my shot or that I can't do this or do that. But I've always said that when my career was over at Michigan State, I just wanted to be remembered as a winner."

He will be.

WHEN IT WAS OVER, MATEEN CLEAVES JUMPED FOR JOY AND FELLOW FLINTSTONE MORRIS PETERSON WAS THERE TO CATCH HIM. "I WANT TO CHERISH THIS MOMENT FOREVER," MOPETE SAID.

JULIAN H. GONZALEZ

Spartans ganged up on the Gators

BY MICHAEL ROSENBERG

ALOYSIUS ANAGONYE

ADAM BALLINGER

MIKE CHAPPELL

STEVE CHERRY

MAT ISHBIA

JASON RICHARDSON

BRANDON SMITH

DAVID THOMAS

They showed up late, and not fashionably late, either. Mind-numbingly, irritatingly late. But when they woke up the morning after — if they ever went to sleep — it didn't matter a bit.

Michigan State's reserves were no-shows at times in the NCAA tournament, but they made up for it in the finale. In the biggest game of the season, the subs might have played their best game of the season.

Without them, the Spartans might have beaten Florida. But it would not have been so easy. It would not have been an 89-76 runaway.

Florida's bench was supposed to be the challenge for Michigan State in the national championship game. The Gators' bench was longer than "War and Peace," and just as impressive. During the season, 10 Gators played significant time, and in their first five NCAA tournament games, Florida led, 175-89, in bench scoring.

But there was Jason Richardson, shooting jumpers, playing defense and sending a loud message that Florida was not the only team with a McDonald's All-American on the bench. Richardson scored nine points.

There was Mike Chappell, hitting a big three-pointer, pretending his season-long slump never happened.

"We ran a play for him there," said Tom Izzo, who said his predecessor,

JULIAN H. GONZALEZ

JASON RICHARDSON, WHO AVERAGED FIVE POINTS A GAME DURING THE SEASON, WAS FLYING HIGH AND FINISHED WITH NINE POINTS AGAINST FLORIDA.

DAVID P. GILKEY

ALOYSIUS ANAGONYE WAS PART OF THE DEFENSIVE WALL THAT KEPT THE GATORS AT BAY.

Jud Heathcote, had told him in mid-season to stick with Chappell despite the slump.

There was Aloysius Anagonye, playing tough defense, setting picks and showing he could do more than get into foul trouble (though he did that, too).

There were David Thomas and Adam Ballinger — yes, David Thomas and Adam Ballinger. They didn't dunk and they didn't drop three-pointers, but their presence was important, and here's why:

Izzo wanted to run against Florida. He felt it was the best way to beat the press — to challenge it, break it apart. He knew he had the athletes to do it.

But MSU could not win a run 'n' gun game with its starters playing 35 minutes each. They would wear down, and that would be fatal. One thing Florida was never going to do was lose because of exhaustion. Ten-deep teams don't have that problem.

Especially in the first half, Izzo substituted as liberally as he has all season. He had to forget that Richardson sometimes had defensive lapses, that Anagonye's shooting was not as refined as Andre Hutson's, that Chappell had struggled with his confidence. Izzo needed them, if only to buy time.

With the frequent substitutions, MSU was always fresh — and never had three or four reserves on the floor for an extended period. And the subs surprised by not merely maintaining leads but extending them.

Richardson scored six points in the first half. Florida's much-hyped bench scored just 11.

The Michigan State subs were so good, by the end of the game the subs' subs were playing.

There were Steve Cherry and Brandon Smith and Mat Ishbia, finishing off what MSU's first and second teams had started.

CHARLIE BELL AND MORRIS PETERSON KNEW THEY WERE CHAMPIONS AS TIME RAN OUT ON FLORIDA IN THE 2000 TITLE GAME.

APRIL 3, 2000
NO. 1 FAN

Phone call from Washington

President Bill Clinton called the Spartans when they entered the locker room after the game, and Charlie Bell answered the phone.

A woman from the White House said, "President Clinton would like to speak to your team." But Bell wasn't buying it.

"Yeah, right," Bell said.

The woman was adamant. "No, President Clinton really wants to talk to you guys."

Bell was put on hold for a few minutes. Then Clinton got on the phone.

Clinton congratulated Tom Izzo and, according to Bell, the players in the background all said in unison, "Hello, Mr. President."

And "that was it," Bell said.

JULIAN H. GONZALEZ

MORRIS PETERSON FELT 10 FEET TALL, BUT HE DIDN'T FORGET THE MEMORY OF HIS LATE GRANDMOTHER, EVEN AS THE TWINE WAS COMING DOWN.

Announcers captured MSU's memorable moment

Free Press sports writer Steve Crowe documented the championship calls from TV and radio:

Jim Nantz, CBS-TV: "They never let go of the dream. And you can leave it to Cleaves. He has reinstated the magic at Michigan State. ... Plant closings, unemployment, poverty, the troubles faced by the residents of Flint, Mich., have been well-documented. But so, too, have the triumphs of their favorite sons, the so-called Flintstones of Michigan State."

Mark Champion, MSU radio network (WXYT-AM): "Brandon Smith with the basketball. Ten seconds. Eight for the championship. Smith to Ballinger. It's five (seconds) — 89-76. Three, two, one — and Michigan State is the national champion! They did it! Peterson and Cleaves hugging down at midcourt! The Michigan State Spartans have won the national championship."

It was never better to be Green

KIRTHMON F. DOZIER

AT THE BRESLIN CENTER:

THOUSANDS GATHERED IN EAST LANSING TO WATCH THE FINALE. HOW DO YOU SPELL CHAMPION? M-S-U.

AT THE RCA DOME:

IN INDIANAPOLIS, IT WAS EASY TO SPOT THE SPARTAN FANS — THEY LOOKED LIKE WINNERS.

ERIC SEALS

BY JAMES G. HILL AND BRIAN MURPHY

This time, students danced in the streets, chanting "M-S-U!" and "Go State!" as the Queen song "We Are the Champions" blared from one student's apartment window. This time, Michigan State really was No. 1.

And long forgotten were the 1999 Final Four loss to Duke and the scenes of burning couches and flying beer cans that followed the loss.

In East Lansing — after the Spartans beat Florida to win the national championship — there was no violence, only celebration. Even the dozens of police officers stationed around Cedar Village, the epicenter of the '99 riot, were handing out high fives instead of tickets.

Across campus, in nearby neighborhoods and in downtown East Lansing, that mood held true. People hung out car windows, high-fiving one another. Police officers leaned out squad car windows shouting, "Go Green!"

"I'm so pleased," said Jessica Sculte, a sophomore from Livonia. "I'm so excited that we're being good sports and celebrating the right way. I'm so proud to be a Spartan right now."

Championship parties reverberated across East Lansing, Flint and anywhere else the green and white gathered.

The MSU faithful had stood in a line that stretched four across and back a quarter-mile to get into the Breslin Center to watch the game on the giant Diamond Vision screen, to clap in unison and to sing the MSU fight song.

"It doesn't get any better than this," Roger Goins, an MSU alum, said as the Spartans took control of the game. "Lightning might not strike in the same place twice, but I'm betting magic does."

KIRTHMON F. DOZIER

AROUND EAST LANSING:

ONE FAN SAID IT ALL: "I'M SO EXCITED THAT WE'RE BEING GOOD SPORTS AND CELEBRATING THE RIGHT WAY. I'M SO PROUD TO BE A SPARTAN RIGHT NOW."

At BW3 in downtown East Lansing, crowds arrived. The beer was green, the atmosphere was electric.

"Just like football!" hundreds of fans chanted, referring to the Spartans' Citrus Bowl win over the Gators.

In Flint, the same spirit prevailed.

The championship game meant as much, if not more, in Flint. Morris Peterson, Mateen Cleaves and Charlie Bell tell the world — with tattoos — that Flint remains their home.

"There's a lot of pride in these young men, and the values their families instilled in them speaks volumes about our community," Flint Schools Superintendent James Ray said. "We are a proud city. And we're going to be a tired city after we're through celebrating."

At Bubba's Roadside Inn, on Flint's west side, businessmen hid starched shirts and ties under green and white sweatshirts while guzzling ale, gulping finger food and cheering alongside college students and grandmothers.

As the final seconds ticked away, Gerald Edwards pulled a cigar from his coat pocket, gnawed off the end and lit the stalest — and sweetest — stogie the Flint native ever smoked.

"I bought this last year when they went to the Final Four," Edwards said. "When they lost to Duke, I decided to keep it because I knew they'd win it this year if they stuck together."

And how did that year-old cigar taste?

"Never better."

TALES OF THE TAPE

Us vs. Them — Charting the battles throughout the tournament

① VALPARAISO

MSU: Previously known as Michigan Agricultural College.
Valpo: Previously known as Valparaiso Male and Female College, and Northern Indiana Normal School and Business Institute.

MSU: Named after the Spartans, the bad boys of ancient Greece.
Valpo: Named after the Crusaders, the bad boys of that thing the pope apologized for.

Valpo: Students' idea of a party is the annual Popcorn Festival in Valparaiso, Ind., and seeing if they can break the local Jaycees' Guinness record for world's largest popcorn ball (12 feet).
MSU: Students' idea of a party is the annual Couch Burning Festival in downtown East Lansing and seeing if they can break open another Guinness (12 ounces).

MSU: Its favorite Stephen King book/movie — "The Green Mile."
Valpo: Its favorite Stephen King book/movie — "Children of the Corn."

MSU: Most crushing loss: to Duke in last year's semifinals.
Valpo: Most crushing loss: The Orville Redenbacher factory is leaving town.

MSU: Players come from Flint, mostly.
Valpo: Players come from exotic places like the Czech Republic, Latvia, Finland, Croatia and Kalamazoo.

② UTAH

They have Utes.
We have Yoopers.

They have Orrin Hatch.
We have Charlie Batch.

They have the Mormon Tabernacle.
We have the Masonic Temple.

They have Monument Valley.
We have Grand Valley.

They have the Bonneville Salt Flats.
We have Flat Rock Speedway.

We have Kid Rock and Madonna.

They have Donny and Marie.

They have the Utah Jazz.
We have the Motown Sound.

They have the Salt Lake City Olympic scandal.
We have the Michigan basketball scandal.

They gave the world Brigham Young.
We gave the world Coleman Young.

They gave the world Scott Mitchell.
We gave the world the Edsel.

③ SYRACUSE

LOCATION:
MSU — On the banks of the Red Cedar in East Lansing, the City Next to the State Capital.
Syracuse — On the Erie Canal in Syracuse, N.Y., the Salt City (be sure to visit the Salt Museum) and hometown of Tom Cruise.

COLORS:
MSU — Green and white.
Syracuse — Only one, orange, at least since 1890. (Before that the school colors were rose pink and pea green, which for some reason weren't popular.)

CAMPUS STATUE:
MSU — The Spartan (a.k.a. Sparty), a 10-foot-6, nearly *au naturel*, ceramic Greek warrior (right).
Syracuse — The Saltine Warrior, a bronze version of the school's previous Native American mascot.

SIDELINE MASCOT:
MSU — Sparty, the full-of-testosterone, jut-jawed, buffest mascot of them all.
Syracuse — Otto, the full-of-vitamin C, not-just-for-breakfast-anymore, plump and juiciest mascot of them all.

ARENA:
MSU — The Breslin Center, which doesn't mean the gang can't shoot straight.
Syracuse — The Carrier Dome, which must make Otto a navel orange.

HOOPS ALUMS:
MSU — Magic Johnson and Steve Smith.
Syracuse — Dave Bing and Derrick Coleman.

FOOTBALL/AUTHOR ALUMS:
MSU — Bubba Smith ("Kill, Bubba, Kill").
Syracuse — Stephen Crane ("The Red Badge of Courage").

FOOTBALL/ACTOR ALUMS:
MSU — Bubba Smith ("Police Academy").
Syracuse — Jim Brown ("The Dirty Dozen," "Mars Attacks!").

④ IOWA STATE

We have Tim Allen.
They have Tom Arnold.

They have Grant Wood.
We have Grant Hill.

We make cars.
They make bacon.

We have General Custer.
They have Buffalo Bill.

They have former Congressman Fred Grandy, who played Gopher on "The Love Boat." | **We have** Michigan State alum Robert Urich, who played the captain on "The Love Boat: The New Wave."

They have Radar O'Reilly and James T. Kirk (the characters, not the actors).
We have Magnum, P.I. and Michigan J. Frog.

We have Sault Ste. Marie.
They have Sioux City.

They have Cedar Rapids.
We have the Red Cedar River.

Not that it matters in this tournament, but we're the Wolverine State and they're the Hawkeye State.
They have Davenport.
And we know what to do with couches, don't we?

⑤ WISCONSIN

They have the beer that made Milwaukee famous.
We have the bridge that made Zilwaukee famous.

They had Laverne and Shirley-brewed Shotz.
We had fire-brewed Stroh's.

They have the Milwaukee Brewers.
We have Phil Garner.

We have Lake Cadillac.
They have Lake Winnebago.

They have Titletown.
We have Hockeytown.

They have Bud Selig.
We have Mike Ilitch.

They have the Wisconsin Dells.
We have the Irish Hills.

They wear cheese on their heads. | **We're** lactose intolerant.

They have Spencer Tracy.
We have Thomas Edison.

They have Harry Houdini.
We have Magic Johnson.

⑥ FLORIDA

They have the Florida Keys.
We have the Soo Locks.

They have the Magic Kingdom.
We have Magic Johnson.

They have Old Sparky.
We have Hall of Fame Sparky.

They have the Panhandle.
We have the Upper Peninsula.

They have Steve Spurrier.
We have Lake Superior.

They have the Okefenokee Swamp.
We have the Detroit Lions.

They have Busch Gardens.
We have Garden City.

They have spring break.
We have March Madness.

They have orange juice.
We have corn flakes.

They wear Gators caps and T-shirts.
We wear alligator belts and shoes.

We have the I-75 starting line.
They have the I-75 finish line.

They have Pavel Bure.
We have Sergei Fedorov.
Who has Anna Kournikova?

They have Elian Gonzalez.
We have Juan Gonzalez.

They have the Citrus Bowl.
We won the Citrus Bowl.

They are Mickey Mouse.
We are the Flintstones.

Great day in East Lansing

JULIAN H. GONZALEZ

AT TOM IZZO'S INVITATION, MUHAMMAD ALI HONORED THE BASKETBALL AND FOOTBALL TEAMS WITH AN APPEARANCE.

BY JEMELE HILL

Champ, say hello to the champs-to-be.
Muhammad Ali met the Spartans in their locker room before they KO'd Connecticut, 85-66, on Feb. 5 at the Breslin Center. Ali's impact on the players was enormous.

"His presence was felt," said Mateen Cleaves, who scribbled "Little Ali" on his gym shoes. "He's the greatest fighter of all time."

Ali had met Tom Izzo previously, and Izzo extended the invitation for Ali to come to a basketball game. It was perfect timing. The Spartans not only won the game, but the Citrus Bowl-champion MSU football team was honored at halftime, as well. Ali came out for a bow during intermission, waving to the crowd and shaking hands with players. Then he posed for pictures with members of the football team and their new coach, Bobby Williams.

Charlie Bell summed it up: "We're trying to be champions, and here we have the greatest champion of all time."

KEVIN W. FOWLER / MSU Sports Information

IN THE COMPANY OF GREATNESS: MATEEN CLEAVES, A.K.A. LITTLE ALI, MEETS THE REAL DEAL.

MEET THE TEAM

It was one big Sparty party — freshmen, seniors, starters and bench players alike — after the victory over Syracuse at the Palace.

THE ROAD TO INDY

Tuesday: Jason Richardson

TOM IZZO

Detroit Free Press

ERIC SEALS

AGE: 45 | 5TH SEASON | COACH | IRON MOUNTAIN

The man from Iron Mountain

BY JO-ANN BARNAS

The words were harsh, coming from a boy so young. He didn't mean it that way. The boy was just being honest, just being Tommy.

As Carl Izzo stared at his son that afternoon more than 30 years ago, he was speechless at first — not an angry speechless, just answerless. Young Tom Izzo sat in the kitchen, a sour expression on his face, his third-grade books stacked on the table. He didn't want to do his homework.

Carl told him: "You want to end up with a pick and shovel for the rest of your life?"

"You quit," Tommy said, "and you ended up all right."

It was true. Carl had left high school early, a few credits shy of a diploma. He was in the service for 26 months during World War II and went to work in his father's business.

So with his son's words, Carl Izzo set out to prove himself. He returned to Iron Mountain High in 1963 and, at age 38, finished what he had started. He got his diploma.

Looking back on the story, at age 74, Carl Izzo could see how it fits neatly into the context of his son's life. Tom Izzo was taking care of some unfinished business of his own — taking the Spartans to the national championship.

Tom Izzo carries with him a lesson learned long ago from his father, a lesson in perseverance. But the boy taught his father something, too. Even at an early age, even when he didn't know it, Tom Izzo had a way of finding the fire in people.

And he hasn't changed. That's what they say about Tom Izzo. Who's they? Try his father, his mother, his wife, his mentor, his best friend, his adviser, his players, his coaching colleagues, his fifth-grade teacher, his Iron Mountain pals, his running

JULIAN H. GONZALEZ

TOM IZZO GETS A HUG FROM HIS MOM, DOROTHY, WITH WIFE, LUPE, BEHIND HIM. CLOSE PERSONAL TIES, IZZO SAYS, ARE HIS LIFELINE. "THEY HELP ME STAY REAL."

partner. Even his 11th-grade basketball coach.

They will all tell you that Izzo hasn't changed a whole lot in the five years since his first season as MSU coach, when he succeeded Jud Heathcote. Izzo's affable boy-nextdoor personality is the same. His passion for organization and detail is the same. His coaching style is pretty much the same. So, too, is his knack for cultivating friendships and hanging on to those special relationships with friends and family up north in Iron Mountain, his hometown.

But things around Izzo have changed. Remember how it was in 1995-96, when MSU lost to Detroit Mercy and Central Michigan in the regular season, finished 16-16 and seventh in the Big Ten? Fan support for Izzo was lukewarm at best.

Now the Spartans have won or tied for the past three Big Ten regu-

lar-season titles. They have become regulars in the NCAA tournament. They have supplanted Michigan as the top basketball team in the state.

"I'll say this now, because I'm sure the day will come when I feel different," Izzo said. "But it's harder to deal with the pressure of success than the pressure of failure. I've been on both sides of the coin, and that's what I've learned. It's been such a whirlwind for me, so many things to deal with.

"That's why I've depended so much on others — I'm not afraid to admit that. It's true that the people who helped raise me, the people that I'm closest to, they've been my lifeline. They help me stay real."

Two stacks of phone messages were arranged in neat piles on Izzo's desk. "I know Jud called, and I was going to call him back at 11 a.m., but the meeting ran late," Izzo said of Heathcote, his mentor, who coached

> "I'll say this now, because I'm sure the day will come when I feel different. But it's harder to deal with the pressure of success than the pressure of failure. I've been on both sides of the coin, and that's what I've learned."
>
> **TOM IZZO**

MSU in 1976-95, winning the 1979 NCAA championship with Gregory Kelser and Magic Johnson.

As close as they were before, Heathcote and Izzo have grown even closer the past couple of years. Heathcote, who hired Izzo as a graduate assistant coach in 1983 for $7,000 a year, calls him "my surrogate son." Heathcote frequently calls, offering old plays to try.

"Every day that goes by, Jud gets smarter to me," Izzo said. "The times I used to say, 'Why is he doing this? Why is he acting that way?' Now I know. I run into the same situations now, and I've stopped myself and said, 'Now I know why Jud did this.' I'm still learning from the past. He's why everybody should have a mentor."

"I look at him now," Heathcote said. "As a person, Tom hasn't changed. Tom's approach to coaching could be summed up with two letters, 'W' and 'W' — work and worry. He's still very humble with the success that he's had. He still sees himself on the bottom of the pile. That's why he's always working so hard."

Tom Izzo is not a complicated man away from basketball. He doesn't smoke. He runs three miles before each game. His wife, Lupe, has never seen him with a cup of coffee. When former players visit, Izzo looks forward to planning something special. So when Antonio Smith popped in to say hello a few months ago, Izzo took Smith and his girlfriend out for ice cream.

"You hear about guys who haven't lost their roots," MSU assistant coach Brian Gregory said. "It's easier said than done, and he's done it. He's constantly trying to bring back people who are important to him. He has to share everything with everyone. One of the principles of his program here has been to instill a family type of atmosphere, and he's done that."

Not surprisingly, when friends and relatives drive the 450 miles from Iron Mountain to East Lansing, they always know they have a place to stay. It's called the Izzo Hotel.

Once, 17 people slept in his basement — the gathering place for most family functions. That's also where Izzo plays the accordion once a year at Christmas.

In December 1991, the basement was the setting of a love story when Izzo got down on one knee and asked Lupe to marry him. There were wit-

nesses, of course — he proposed in front of 50 family members and friends. The Izzos have one daughter, Raquel. This past year, Lupe said she mailed 500 Christmas cards.

"Everyone knows he's a strait-laced guy — always was," said Izzo's best friend, Steve Mariucci, coach of the San Francisco 49ers. "He hasn't changed one bit." On Izzo's 18th birthday, Mariucci remembers how they celebrated: two bottles of 7-Up. "We didn't drink," Mariucci said. "It was a funny way to say, 'It's OK.'"

Born Jan. 30, 1955, in Iron Mountain — the oldest and only son of Carl and Dorothy Izzo's three children — Tom grew up in a town where family and hard work meant nearly the same thing. The family business — started by Tom's grandfather — was called Izzo Shoe Hospital.

"But with five kids, there wasn't enough shoe repairing for everybody, so we branched out into home repairing and other things," Carl Izzo said. "Now my youngest brother owns the shoe repair, I got the awning shop, and my brother, Ralph, has the carpeting. We're all in one building, but with separate

THERESA PETERSON/Iron Mountain Daily News

entrances. So on the side of the building it says 'Tony Izzo & Sons & Grandsons.' "

As a youngster, Tom Izzo worked in most of the shops. He began at about age 12, handing his father tools. But Carl Izzo knew when Tom was young that he wouldn't stay in the family business.

"Before he left for Michigan State in 1983, I told him that I would hand him the keys if he wanted it," Carl Izzo said of the business. "But I knew he had a dream to get."

But Tom Izzo, he never forgets. "The cornerstone of everything in my life — from the players to the people up north — is that I will never be above them," Izzo said. "That's why I end 90 percent of our practices the same way. I say, 'Whatever you did today, whatever you put in, you'll get back exactly what you deserve.'

"I never want my theory blown. I never want to get something for nothing."

HOMETOWN HEROES

Tom Izzo and San Francisco 49ers coach Steve Mariucci grew up together in Iron Mountain. They played high school football and basketball together in the early '70s. They were roommates and walk-ons in their respective sports at Northern Michigan. Both went on to earn Division II All-America honors.

Each year, Izzo and Mariucci co-host a golf tournament in Iron Mountain to raise money for the community. Heck, they even served as best man at each other's wedding. ("He married way over his head," Mariucci says.)

Mariucci could write a book about his old pal, and, in a way, he has. "I put his stuff in my scrapbook," said

JIM PATTERSON / Special to the Free Press

AN IRON-CLAD FRIENDSHIP: TOM IZZO AND STEVE MARIUCCI (ABOVE).

Mariucci, who has been collecting news clippings on his buddy for as long as he can remember.

Mariucci sums up their friendship this way: "He is just an everyday, all-of-the-time type of best friend. Not just at the class reunion or through Christmas cards. We're connected a little bit more than friends."

Tom Izzo

It was their shining moment

BY DREW SHARP

The Final Four is about snapshots, memories from the instant of impending victory forever frozen in our thoughts and hearts. It's the "One Shining Moment" CBS sings about during its tournament coverage.

Before the semifinals, Mateen Cleaves talked about what it would be like to walk off the court for the last time as a Spartan and greet his coach, combatant and confidant of the four years, Tom Izzo.

"Win or lose, it's going to be an emotional moment because it'll be the end of a long road for us," Cleaves said. "I'm sure there's going to be some tears because we've both been through so much together. But, man, if we win, he's going to get the biggest bear hug he's ever gotten in his life."

It's been a peculiar alliance — two volatile personalities from diverse backgrounds embracing each other's ambitions to build something memorable from the mediocrity that was Michigan State basketball when Izzo took over in 1995.

The road wasn't without potholes. They clashed often, one challenging the limits of the other's tolerance to see how far he could push before the other pushed back. But each learned from the other, ultimately forging a respect that grew in direct proportion

PRELUDE TO A NATIONAL CHAMPIONSHIP KISS: TOM IZZO AND MATEEN CLEAVES AT THE BRESLIN CENTER FINALE.

JULIAN H. GONZALEZ

TOM IZZO AND MATEEN CLEAVES HAD MSU POINTED IN THE RIGHT DIRECTION.

with the success of the program.

"But we've had our moments," Izzo recalled.

One of them came in the aftermath of the Spartans' loss at Kentucky on Dec. 23. Cleaves believed he was ready to return from his fractured foot and demanded to play, if only sparingly, in the Spartans' last two non-conference games. Izzo thought otherwise, believing it was best Cleaves wait another week.

Angry, Cleaves told Izzo that if he wasn't allowed to play, he would stop going to class. Through the years, Cleaves learned the right buttons to push to ignite Izzo's internal volcano, and blowing off class was one of them. But Izzo didn't bite. There was no eruption this time. Instead, Izzo used an argument Cleaves couldn't rebut — winning above all else.

How would Cleaves feel if a premature return hurt the team in the long run?

"He knew Mateen was frustrated over not being able to play, so he made him understand the importance of making sure he was completely healthy," said Frances Cleaves, Mateen's mother. "And then he got into Mateen's face and told him he was going to class or else."

Or else what?

"Or else Mateen was going to have to tell ME that he wasn't going to class anymore," his mother said.

Izzo will miss Cleaves. "Mateen has taught me that if a coach expects his players to go to the wall for him when things get tough on the court, then the coach had better be prepared to go to the wall for his players when things get tough for them off the court," Izzo said. "Our relationship has helped make me a better coach and, more important, a better person because it made me understand the importance of looking beneath the exterior to see what's really important deep down."

And Cleaves will miss Izzo. He's even going to miss those late-night phone calls.

"Coach is the kind of guy that whenever something comes into his head, he's telling me about it," Cleaves said. "The phone rang one time at 1 in the morning, and he was calling to tell me about something he read about people taking shots at our program. He kept saying to me: 'It's time, Mo. It's time.' And I told him it is time, Coach. It's time for me to get back to sleep."

THE ROAD TO INDY

Tuesday: Morris Peterson

Mateen
CLEAVES

Detroit Free Press

NO. 12 | SENIOR | POINT GUARD | FLINT NORTHERN

Never fear, Mateen's here

JULIAN H. GONZALEZ

MATEEN CLEAVES' PARENTS ALWAYS ENCOURAGED HIM TO BE A LEADER, AND HE MIGHT HAVE BEEN THE GREATEST THE SPARTANS EVER HAD.

BY JEMELE HILL

All the other kids were jumping into the swimming pool, so 5-year-old Mateen Cleaves didn't see why he couldn't do it, too. He sucked in his breath, leaped in and . . . sank.

"I was a young chance-taker back in my time," Cleaves said.

His father, Herbert Cleaves, jumped in that day and pulled Mateen to the surface. Afterward, Mateen's mother, Frances, said: "That little bugger was sitting there screaming and hollering to go back in. He went in because the other kids went in. My immediate thought was, 'Oh, boy, he's going to be afraid of water now.' "

Not Mateen Cleaves. From the day he was born, his parents taught him not to be fearful. And 22 years later, he has staked a claim as one of the best players in school history. Cleaves holds several records — most assists in Big Ten history, most steals at Michigan State — but more important is his leadership.

Cleaves might be MSU's greatest

JULIAN H. GONZALEZ

REGULAR SEASON OR TOURNEY TIME, CLEAVES WORKED HARD. "HE DOESN'T TAKE PRACTICES OFF," IZZO SAID.

leader ever, and that's saying a lot at Magic Johnson's school.

"I honestly think he is," said Tom Izzo, who was first hired at Michigan State in 1983, as a graduate assistant coach. "There have been great leaders by example. There have been great vocal leaders. Few do both."

Where did it all start?

Cleaves was a surprise and a miracle. When he came along, Frances and Herbert Cleaves, now divorced, had four children: three boys and a girl. But before that, Frances had two stillborns and two miscarriages.

"Mateen was really a blessing," she said.

A Muslim minister suggested the name, which means "strength, intelligence and fierce."

Frances and Herbert Cleaves wanted their children to be leaders, to be the sort who would speak up and not be afraid of a battle. So the Cleaves children were taken places where battles were fought: protests, marches, picket lines, school board meetings.

When Mateen was 5, he was in a neighborhood cleanup group that planted flowers along run-down streets in Flint. That same year, he marched in a parade to celebrate the birthday of Dr. Martin Luther King Jr. The first time he was photographed in a newspaper, he didn't have a basketball in his hand. He was standing among a sea of marchers, holding a sign that was nearly bigger than he was. It read: "Happy B-Day Martin Luther King."

A year later, Cleaves was on the picket lines with his parents, protesting to save jobs at a General Motors plant where his mother worked for 22 years before retiring in 1998.

"I remember going to union meetings and marches," Cleaves said. "It's helped me out. I'm still into that kind of stuff. If it's a civil rights movie on, I'm sitting there watching it. That helped me out so far as my communication skills, being around people and being the strong person that I am."

"I tried to teach all of my kids they were a part of a greater community, and that everybody has to play a part in making it better for everybody else," Frances Cleaves said. "And that has a lot to do with him being a good team player. You never hear him making comments about being better than other people."

When Herbert Cleaves, a community liaison with the Genesee County Community Action Agency, saw his son showing an interest in basketball at a young age, he showed him the championship football ring he had won at Flint Northern in 1960, the last state championship football team at the school.

Cleaves takes pride that he and his son won state titles at Flint Northern, the son's coming in basketball. "How many homes can you go around where the father and son went to the same high school and won championships?" he said.

Izzo is quick to call Cleaves not only his best player, but also the hardest-working. "Mateen has very few bad practices," Izzo said. "He doesn't take practices off. When that guy is gone, I'm going to find out if I can really coach."

In March, Cleaves and teammate Morris Peterson were voted second-team All-Americas. "I don't get caught up in all of that," said Cleaves, repeating a line he often uses. "I don't get caught up in the individual stuff. I just want to be remembered as a winner."

Battling buddies

EVERY DAY IN PRACTICE, BRANDON SMITH CHALLENGED HIS FRIEND AND MADE HIM A BETTER PLAYER.

JULIAN H. GONZALEZ

BY JEMELE HILL

This time, the casualty was Brandon Smith's nose. The Spartans were practicing before the national semifinal game against Wisconsin, and dried blood was stuck to Smith's upper lip, a war wound courtesy of Mateen Cleaves.

Cleaves — unhappy with the way he was being guarded — popped Smith, then called out, "Next time, stop holding me."

These two teammates have said worse to one another, and each has incurred his share of scrapes, bruises and bloody noses. Their exchanges in practice, at least the G-rated ones, usually go something like this:

Mateen: "You can't play with me."

Brandon: "I'm taking the ball from you."

Mateen: "Go ahead and try."

Daily, they claw at each other like enemies. Then, once the horn blows to end practice, Cleaves and Smith laugh with each other like little boys at a slumber party. Another day, another war.

A lot of people helped make Cleaves a better player. But the person who rarely receives credit for his development is Smith, the little-known, little-used reserve who irritates Cleaves every day.

"I might come into practice feeling lazy and tired," Cleaves said, "but then there's Brandon slapping the floor and saying, 'Let's go.'"

"Mateen will have to push Brandon off of him just to get a shot off," Andre Hutson said. "It's a normal thing. But we don't have any egos on this team. We treat each other as equals. We're that way on the floor, and then we go in the locker room and ask, 'What's going on

tonight?'"

Cleaves and Smith have little in common — other than friendship.

Cleaves, the senior team leader from Flint Northern, is a two-time All-America and Big Ten player of the year, one of the most celebrated athletes in Michigan State's history. He's a communications major who loves to communicate boisterously.

Smith, a junior from Rochester, N.Y., has played little more than 100 minutes all season. He's a transfer from Coastal Carolina who came to Michigan State and walked on. He's a microbiology student who dreams of becoming a dentist after he's done playing basketball.

Yet they were roommates for a summer.

"I'm a little bit more reserved," Smith said. "He's a little bit more audacious. But when we're together, anywhere, we're equals. There's no difference because he's a real successful person."

Their friendship was forged when Smith arrived in 1997. Smith was shy but was brought out of his shell by Cleaves, who insisted they hang out together. The friendship grew, but so did their competitiveness. And not just in basketball.

Cards: "I say I'm better," Smith said.

Cleaves shook his head and smiled broadly. "They say I cheat at cards, but I'm a winner. It's not cheating unless you get caught."

Basketball?

"I'm a little better ballhandler," Smith said. "I'm a little quicker. Back in New York, all we do is dribble."

Cleaves: "I tell him, 'You won't stop me.'"

Dates? Smith politely deferred. "I can't compete there," he said. "He's the star."

THE ROAD TO INDY

Wednesday: A.J. Granger

MO
O
PETERSON

Detroit Free Press

NO. 42 | SENIOR | FORWARD | FLINT NORTHWESTERN

Challenged to be a champion

BY JEMELE HILL

JULIAN H. GONZALEZ

WHEN PUSH CAME TO SHOVE, MORRIS PETERSON RESPONDED.

Morris Peterson grew into a national champion, but he didn't start out that way.

The stories begin during Peterson's childhood, when he was prone to take the easy way out. One recollection: Peterson's father, Morris Sr., told his son to rake the leaves, but the leaves went untouched. So at 1 a.m., Morris Sr. woke up his son and made him rake the leaves.

But his son learned slowly.

When Peterson was a freshman at MSU, he skipped so many classes that Tom Izzo left him at home when the team went to Hawaii for the Maui Invitational. Peterson played only four games that season and was declared a medical redshirt after suffering a broken finger.

But two years later, another injury started his turnaround. Peterson, a left-hander, suffered a broken bone in his right wrist, and for most of the season he wore a cast. That's when "I just tried to make myself into the person and player I knew I could be," he said.

Assistant coach Stan Heath has seen Peterson blossom.

"Whenever he was told he was weak in one area, he's responded," Heath said. "When I first got here, I used to say, 'You can't go right. You can't make a right-hand lay-up.' He just gives you that look and nods and says, 'OK, I'm going to show you.' " And he has.

Peterson also gets a push from an unlikely source — student manager Stephen Finamore, who puts a crumpled slip of paper into one of Peterson's basketball shoes before a game. On the slips are nuggets of information meant to rile him.

Before Peterson scored 31 points against North Carolina, Finamore's message reminded him that the Tar Heels hadn't lost a home opener since 1928. And before a career-high 32 points against Michigan, Finamore reminded him that no Michigan State player had scored 30 against the Wolverines since Shawn Respert hit for 33

in 1995. Finamore boldly wrote: "Can you Credit Mateen Cleaves, too, for a share of Peterson's growth. Cleaves, Peterson's roommate and close friend, has two primary jobs: running the offense and needling Peterson.

"I'm always on him because I want him to be the best he can be," Cleaves said. "I want him to get everything out of it he can get."

"Any athlete can make $100 million," said Morris Sr., an assistant principal at Flint's Schools of Choice. "If you don't have a sense of responsibility, it will slip away from you anyway."

Though Peterson had to rake leaves in the early hours, he finally got the message and now says: "My father is my role model. He didn't tolerate any nonsense."

Mr. Morris: "He's my buddy"

BY JEMELE HILL

Fitting the last piece of the Little Mermaid puzzle seemed harder than hitting a three-pointer from the corner. Mr. Morris tried to squeeze it in anyway, until a pair of tiny hands overtook his bumbling effort and slid the piece in easily.

"See, you're doing it all by yourself," Mr. Morris said to the little genius, 2-year-old Antonio Thompson. "I have to practice," Antonio replied. "I guess I have to practice, too," Mr. Morris said.

Mr. Morris is the most famous intern ever at the Parkwood branch of the YMCA of Metropolitan Lansing. He's also the only intern to have been voted Big Ten basketball player of the year.

Morris Peterson is known as Mr. Morris by the children who frequent the community center. To the staff and organizers there, he's another Michigan State intern compiling 270 service hours in order to earn his community and family services degree, and a man who aspires to run his own community center one day.

Peterson goes from sinking three-pointers, running the fast break and rebounding to mopping the YMCA floors, serving preschoolers doughnuts and apple juice, and attending YMCA board meetings to learn the financial aspects of running a commu-

CRAIG PORTER

BEFORE MSU PLAYED AT THE PALACE, MOPETE TOOK TIME OUT FROM BASKETBALL IN BRACKETVILLE TO SPEND TIME WITH THE KIDS AT THE YMCA OF METROPOLITAN LANSING.

"I saw the impact both my parents had on kids, and I wanted
to do that. People 30 years old will come up to me and say,
'Your father helped me out so much. He's my favorite teacher.' "
MORRIS PETERSON

CRAIG PORTER

THE KIDS DIG MR. MORRIS. "THEY CAN'T GET ENOUGH OF HIM," A CO-WORKER SAYS.

nity organization.

One day during the NCAA tournament, he spent three hours at the Y. That night, he spent a few more hours at the Palace, where the Spartans eliminated Syracuse.

"We're trying to give him hands-on experience," said Scott Goldstein, executive director of the center. "He's a celebrity in town, but I'm trying to keep it on an internship level. We're trying to treat him like any other intern."

Peterson comes from a family of educators. His mother, Valarie, teaches at a Flint middle school. His father, Morris Sr., is an administrator.

"I saw the impact both my parents had on kids, and I wanted to do that," Peterson said. "People 30 years old will come up to me and say, 'Your father helped me out so much. He's my favorite teacher.' "

It must run in the family. Peterson receives similar praise at the Y.

"He's so good with the kids," said Julie Green, who has worked at the YMCA for 5½ years. "They can't get enough of him. They hang all over him.

"My 5-year-old son, Dillon, took a picture with him. He met him one time. He saw him on television and said, 'That's Mr. Morris. He's my buddy.' "

THE ROAD TO INDY

Thursday: Andre Hutson

A.J.
GRANGER

Detroit Free Press

NO. 43 | SENIOR | FORWARD | FINDLAY (OHIO) LIBERTY-BENTON

Taking care of business

BY MITCH ALBOM

Oh, sure, that might have been fun. Different girlfriend every week. Being a "player" on the party scene. Might have been fun. Just wasn't him. Not A. J. Granger.

When he arrived as a freshman at Michigan State, he already had a high school sweetheart. And after he graduates, he's going to marry her. Same girl. "The other guys on the team can't believe it," he admits. "They keep saying to me, now you got four months left as a single man, now you got three months left."

Granger shrugs it off. This is who he is, he says. His father married young, raised a loving family. Now it's the son's turn. A. J. gave his girlfriend a ring when he was just a sophomore.

"We've even talked about the whole kid thing already."

Kids? He's 21. Nowadays, that is a kid. But not so long ago, it wasn't. Not so long ago, to be a graduating senior from college, with a sweetheart, and a wedding date and long-range plans for kids was perfectly normal.

A. J. Granger was just born behind his time.

So while his teammates take calls from friends wanting tickets, Granger takes calls from his fiance, Heather Wilhelm, who tells him about the catering, the invitations, the tablecloths and the guest list for the wedding.

And while other guys dream about a party-soaked summer, Granger has a day in late July circled, the day he becomes a husband and his fiance becomes his wife.

"Didn't you ever hear of sowing your wild oats?" he is asked. "I heard of it," he said. Just wasn't him.

Oh, sure, skipping class might have been fun. Taking a light workload. Staying out late. Sleeping in most mornings, letting the incompletes pile up, skating just over the minimum academic requirements to stay eligible for the important thing: basketball. Lots of athletes do it. But it just wasn't him. Not A. J. Granger.

From the start, he paced his academics the way a marathoner paces his steps. He never fell behind in credits. In the summer, when he stuck around to work on his game, he took classes as well.

He picked a major (marketing) and stayed with it, unlike players who jump majors regularly. As a result, he's not only going to graduate after four years, right on schedule, he's taking a light load this semester because he doesn't need any more credits.

"A lot of players, I guess, don't want to mess up their summers with summer school," he said, "but that's what you have to do."

And while other college athletes act as if academics are a burden, and, oh, by the way, terribly unfair, Granger will march across the stage to get his diploma, with nearly a B average, despite all the games, practices, road trips, film sessions and interviews.

"But isn't it true," he is asked, "that many players say it's nearly impossible to study and play college sports?" "Yeah, they say that," he says. Just isn't him.

So, sure, you're thinking the guy goes to classes, the guy is graduating in four years, the guy is getting married: He must not be much of a player. Wrong. Granger has overcome everything from mononucleosis to the near-paralysis of his father in a swimming accident and become an integral cog in MSU's wheel.

He is a starter. He is steady. He has even become a pro prospect. And as for fun? "Don't you feel bad when your schoolmates go on spring break, and they party and jump on tables and do wet T-shirt contests?" he is asked.

"Well, I see it this way," he says. "They get to do some things I'm not getting to do, but I get to do things they'll never do. I've got three (Big Ten) rings on my fingers. Besides, we danced on tables when we've won big games." He laughs. "And our T-shirts were wet, too."

Most of the time the world moves too fast, college kids seem to come from another planet, nothing they want is what we wanted, everything they want we deem foolish or insignificant. And then along comes a throwback, a lanky, brown-haired, toothy-grinned senior who looks at times as if he wandered in from the Amish country — but is actually the best kind of hope for college athletics.

Hardworking. Graduating. On time. And about to become a husband.

"I'm lucky my fiance is so good about taking care of the details," he says. "Except the honeymoon."

Why not the honeymoon?

"That's my department."

What'd you think? The guy wasn't going to have any fun?

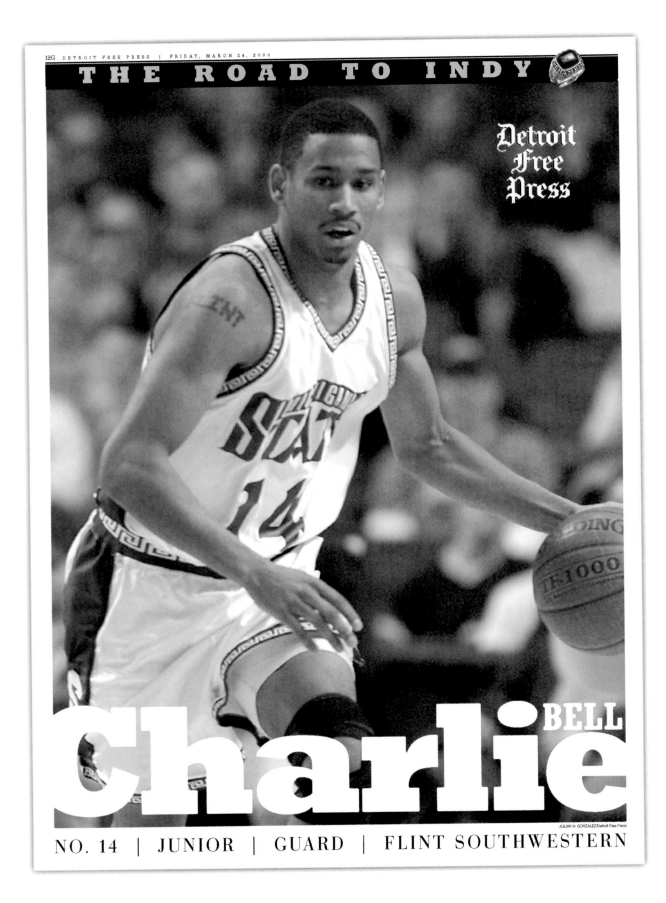

THE ROAD TO INDY

Detroit
Free
Press

JULIAN H. GONZALEZ/Detroit Free Press

Charlie BELL

NO. 14 | JUNIOR | GUARD | FLINT SOUTHWESTERN

Charlie Bell, David Thomas do their homework

BY JEMELE HILL

One young woman thought he was beautiful, thought he looked perfect in his basketball shorts, proposed marriage using a sign at a basketball game.

And Kenya Howard — Charlie Bell's girlfriend — laughed. A lot of women want her boyfriend's attention, and she has become accustomed to the silly and outlandish offers.

"There are a lot of women that are attracted to him," Howard said. "I can put up with it because of the way Charlie is. He'll let me know and let me read his e-mails. A lot of it is funny."

Relationships aren't easy, and it gets more complicated when fame, admiring women and inflexible schedules are mixed in.

"There are pros and cons to being with someone who plays basketball," said Toni Nelson, a physical therapy major at MSU and girlfriend of David Thomas.

The benefits depend largely on the athletes involved. Howard and Nelson give their boyfriends glowing endorsements. And it seems these players are natural romantics.

How many other boyfriends could promise this?

"Charlie told me he was going to score 20 points for me for Valentine's Day," Howard said. And it wasn't an empty promise. The Spartans beat Ohio State, 83-72, the day after Valentine's Day, and Bell scored 23.

Another benefit is travel. Howard has been to all but one road game, and Nelson and Howard traveled with the team to Puerto Rico during Thanksgiving break.

But let's not forget another advantage — hey, you're dating an MSU basketball player!

"I have to be honest, when I was a freshman, I thought it was so cool," said Nelson. But there are negatives.

JULIAN H. GONZALEZ

SO YOU WANT TO DATE A BASKETBALL STAR? DATING A SPARTAN LIKE CHARLIE BELL MEANS DEALING WITH A CRAZY SCHEDULE AND CRAZY FANS.

At the top of the list: lack of time.

Players don't have a lot of it during the season, especially when they play for Tom Izzo and contend for the national title.

"I can't say I'm used to it yet," Nelson said. Most days, she doesn't talk to Thomas until late at night. With her schoolwork, his practices and games, they might be lucky to get one day to themselves a week.

And then there's the misconception that all athletes are playboys.

Morris Peterson reluctantly admitted he has been shot down a few times because of it. "People don't want to talk to you because they say, 'You're an athlete, and you know how athletes are.'"

Bell and Thomas have worked hard to combat that image. And their girlfriends have worked equally hard to make their guys understand they weren't there just for the thrills of being with a basketball star. Even if he does score 20 points for Valentine's Day.

Jason
RICHARDSON

Detroit
Free
Press

NO. 23 | FRESHMAN | FORWAR

JULIAN H. GONZALEZ/*Detroit Free Press*

SAGINAW ARTHUR HILL

Doing what comes naturally

BY JEMELE HILL

The kid, a ninth-grader, was in a gym, dressed in blue jeans and boat shoes, dunking.

In boat shoes. And with as much ease as a chef flipping a pancake.

"I couldn't believe he was doing it," said Greg McMath, an assistant coach at Saginaw Arthur Hill, where the kid played high school ball. "That's when I knew this kid is going to be special."

The kid is Jason Richardson, also known as Dominique Wilkins, also known as the Human Highlight, also known as the player who can do the extraordinary above the rim.

"It's just a natural instinct," Richardson said. "Morris Peterson shoots a three-pointer, and that's natural to him. Dunking is natural to me."

Richardson came up with two of the best plays of the regular season. Against North Carolina, Richardson drove the length of the court, put a wicked crossover move on 7-footer Brendan Haywood (who toppled to the floor), and finished it with a rim-rattling, one-hand dunk.

Then, at Arizona, Richardson made ESPN's plays of the week with a reverse put-back dunk. "That should be an ESPY," Mateen Cleaves said. "He's the best athlete in the country. You pray and hope he gets alone on a fast break.

"I saw him walk up to the rim and do a windmill. He put it between his legs and dunked it. He's one of those guys who will make a decent point guard look like an All-America," said Cleaves, who tagged the freshman with a nickname — "Bones."

Richardson, 6-feet-6, 215 pounds, explained: "He said I'm skinny and I need to hit the weight room."

THE ROAD TO INDY

Thursday: Mike Chappell

ALOYSIUS Anagonye

Detroit Free Press

NO. 25 | FRESHMAN | CENTER | DETROIT DEPORRES

Spartans tackle a tough assignment

BY MICK McCABE

The day after their 21-game Big Ten winning streak was snapped at Ohio State, the Spartans had a surprise waiting for them at practice. On a table were eight football helmets, eight sets of shoulder pads and eight jerseys.

Welcome to Tom Izzo's brand of basketbrawl.

The night before, the Spartans were not as aggressive as they had been earlier in the season, and Izzo was determined to regain that edge. So he sent equipment manager Dave Pruder to the Duffy Daugherty Football Building to fetch some equipment.

The moment Mateen Cleaves saw the equipment, he raced over to the table. "Give me that helmet!" he shouted.

"Wait a minute, you're not going to wear that," Izzo said. "You're not in this drill."

"Oh, yes I am," Cleaves said as he put on a helmet and grabbed a pair of shoulder pads.

Once dressed, the players began to play War, the name for a daily rebounding drill. But this time it had a twist — football equipment. And getting everyone dressed was an adventure in itself.

"It was funny watching some of the guys," Cleaves said. "It took them a half-hour to get dressed. The guys who never played football didn't know what went where."

One of those needing assistance was senior forward A. J. Granger. "I went over to Mateen and asked him how to put on the shoulder pads," Granger said. "I didn't know where anything snapped."

Izzo, a standout prep football player at Iron Mountain, calls the drill "War." Charlie Bell describes it as "a box-out drill, and it's no-holds-barred. You can do anything you have to do."

But some players had an advantage. Cleaves, an all-state quarterback and defensive back at Flint Northern, made the Free Press Best of the Midwest team as one of the top football prospects in the Midwest.

Andre Hutson, a high school quarterback in Ohio, was recruited by Ohio State until he gave up the game. Freshman Jason Andreas was a tight end and defensive end in high school in Ohio.

Aloysius Anagonye, 6-feet-8, 250 pounds, most resembles a football player among the Spartans. But he played the sport only one year at Detroit DePorres.

"I was a soccer player when I was little," said Anagonye, who probably didn't need the pads but wore them anyway.

With Cleaves setting the tone, MSU players jumped into the drill with a lot of enthusiasm, even those who had no football experience.

"I took a couple of people down," Bell said. "I got a couple of floor burns, but I made it out alive."

Mike Chappell played youth football in Southfield but hadn't put on pads in years. "That was the closest I got to Division I football," Chappell said. "And that was the closest I ever want to get to Division I football."

Coaches often borrow ideas from other coaches, but this was an Izzo original.

"Hell, some people probably thought I was nuts," Izzo said. "I didn't think we were rebounding like we should. The best thing that happened is we had some fun. And we needed fun that day."

BIG MEN ON CAMPUS: ALOYSIUS ANAGONYE (OPPOSITE) AND SPARTY.

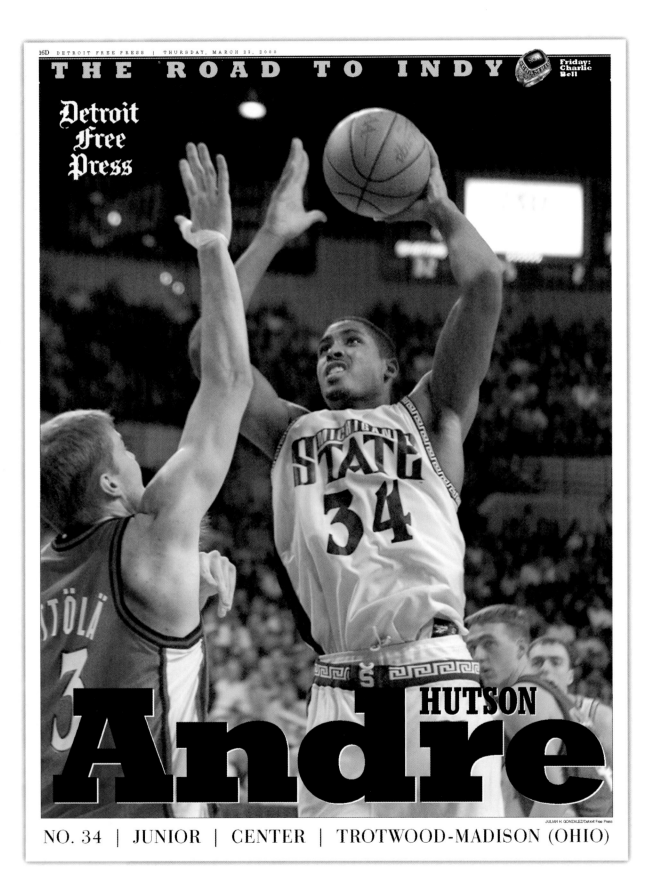

THE ROAD TO INDY

Friday: Charlie Bell

Detroit Free Press

STATE 34

TÖLÄ 3

Andre HUTSON

JULIAN H. GONZALEZ/Detroit Free Press

NO. 34 | JUNIOR | CENTER | TROTWOOD-MADISON (OHIO)

Someone to look up to

BY MITCH ALBOM

She was barely 17 years old, and she was pregnant. This was not what she had in mind. What about high school? What about college? What about her track and field career? A baby?

"This can't be," she told her mother.

"It is," her mother said, gently. "You made a mistake, and now you have to turn it into something positive."

The son was born. She gave him his father's name, Andre Hutson, in an effort to make the man feel more responsible for his child.

It didn't quite work.

So she raised him by herself, with help from her mother, and she did the best she could. And when the boy was 10 years old, he said, "I want a baby sister! Can we have one?"

Another baby, she thought? That's the last thing I need. Being a single mom is hard enough with one. But then came this little girl, a foster child, and the baby looked into her son's eyes, and they were special eyes.

This is a story about hands, the hand you're dealt, and the hand you offer.

Andre Hutson grew up and helped lead the Spartans to a national championship. And Andre's mother, Linda Morris, was there, rooting lovingly for the hand she was dealt. And next to her was 12-year-old Kristyn, the baby sister Andre always wanted. Once a foster child, unwanted by her natural parents, she now has green-and-white shirts, green-and-white hats, green-and-white pennants, and, locked away in her house, the Final Four ring that Andre got in the 1999 tournament. It is hers. A gift from her older brother.

Who came into her life because a hand was offered.

"My little sister's cool," Hutson

JULIAN H. GONZALEZ

ANDRE HUTSON MAKES A LOT OF NOISE — ON THE COURT. OFF THE COURT, IT'S A DIFFERENT STORY.

said. "When I was a kid I always wanted someone to pick on. But now she looks up to me, and she tries to get up to campus and hang out with me all the time."

Well, why not? Hutson is living the life, isn't he? The star big man on the best team in the country? Who wouldn't want to hang around that? And yet, there is no star ego here. No megaphones in Andre Hutson's hands. Mateen Cleaves does the talking. Morris Peterson backs him up.

Hutson is the perfect symbol for this Spartans team — for his perseverance, his workmanlike approach and his low volume.

"I never believed in making noise," said Linda Morris, from Trotwood, Ohio, where Andre grew up. "I tend to emphasize being polite, soft-spo-

ken. That's how most of the folks in my family are. We're not aggressive people. We don't fight over food or anything. We deal with things."

Like a baby at age 17. Like an apartment that was too small. Like having to go to school in the hours around her family's needs — which Linda did, managing to earn an associate degree and then a bachelor's degree through work, sweat, late nights and early mornings.

"My family life has worked out pretty well," Hutson said, smiling. "My grandmother is a hard worker, she passed that on to my mom, and it got passed on to me — and my sister.

"Besides," he said, "my mom is really young-looking. The first time I came to Michigan State, the guys on the team kept thinking she was my sister. They said, 'Man, your mom's cute.'

"It's hard to believe at my age now — 21 — my mom already had me and I was four years old," Hutson said. "But she's talked to me about that. She's told me to be careful out here, that there are a lot of girls who might be interested in me for the wrong reasons, for status and stuff. And I never want to do anything to disappoint her, because she did such a good job of raising me."

You want to know why the fans swoon over this Michigan State team? Because when you look at the Spartans, playing, soaring, laughing, jamming, sweating on defense, flying on offense, you don't just see a bunch of kids out for stats or TV time. You see the layers behind them.

Hutson is a prime example. Came into the world by accident. Landed on a cushion of love and guidance. Now is passing it on to a kid sister, who also came into the world with the deck stacked against her.

A hand was offered. And a family was born.

THE ROAD TO INDY · FRIDAY: COLLECTOR SPECIAL

MIKE Chappell

Detroit Free Press

NO. 20 | JUNIOR | FORWARD | SOUTHFIELD-LATHRUP

The Blue Devil who turned Green

BY MITCH ALBOM

When the Spartans left for the Final Four, most of them were thinking about glory and championships. One of them was thinking about the bus ride. And the plane ride. And the locker room.

And it made him nearly as happy as hitting a winning jumper. "I may run home and get my camcorder, just to film all the little stuff," he said.

Mike Chappell belongs. Oh, he may not have had the greatest season. But he's part of it. He's inside. In 1999, when the Spartans went to the Big Dance, Chappell went stag. Because he had transferred from Duke, he was forced to sit out the season and forbidden to participate in most team activities.

So, come Final Four time, Chappell couldn't travel with the Spartans. He had to buy a plane ticket. And he couldn't ride the team bus, so he and his parents shared a cab. He was allowed to hang out at the team hotel, but he couldn't sleep there. So at the end of the evenings — when the fun really got started, when buddies like Mateen Cleaves and Morris Peterson were in their rooms, sharing the midnight talk, laughing at some stupid joke, throwing things across the beds, being everything college kids get to be — Chappell went back to his hotel room across town, like a tourist.

He was the insider on the outside. A kid with his nose to the window. To make matters worse, MSU's opponent in the semifinals was — who else? — Duke. Chappell watched his old teammates battle his new team-mates — not from either bench, but from the stands.

Talk about a man without a country.

"When I was a kid, I used to write lists of my goals and put them on my walls," said Chappell, a lean, sleek-looking forward, designed for shooting, which is his specialty. "I knew what I wanted to accomplish when I was in eighth grade, ninth grade, 10th grade."

And for a while, it seemed as if his roller coaster would never dip. Chappell grew to 6-feet-9 and became a big star at Southfield-Lathrup, good enough to not only be pursued by major universities, but to have his pick.

So instead of choosing nearby Michigan or Michigan State, he selected Duke. After all, only the really special players get to go there, right? "I was young and maybe I was caught up in the appeal of playing there," he admitted. "I thought it was too good an opportunity to pass up."

For a while, he seemed correct. As a starter for Mike Krzyzewski, he was often praised by the coach. Then things changed. His playing time diminished. His output dimmed. He was like a flashlight losing battery strength.

Duke recruited Corey Maggette, who everyone knew was going to be a major star, and he could play Chappell's position. At the end of his sophomore year, Chappell decided he wanted out. He wanted to come home.

He transferred to MSU. Which, of course, meant a year of sitting around, not playing. NCAA policy.

So Chappell sat around East Lansing, being part of the team but not on the team. Celebrating without contributing. During games — such as the '99 Final Four — he was dry and dressed, and, as any athlete will tell you, if you don't break a sweat, you don't feel involved.

All that, of course, was supposed to go away this season. A breakout year for the hometown kid. Everyone remembered Chappell as a high school hero and hoped he could bring that talent to an already loaded team — but it didn't work out that way. Chappell started slowly and never hit stride. For most of the season, he didn't even average seven points, and his shooting — always his trump card — was off.

"I think I was my own worst enemy," he said. "I set goals so high they were impossible to reach. I started feeling like I was letting everyone down around me, and then it feels like the weight of the world is on you. Then you start thinking too much, second-guessing yourself on the court."

Slowly, he began to emerge from that funk. His shooting improved with his confidence and attitude. The young boy inside of him grew up. He realized you don't always hit the goals on that piece of paper. But you have to go on.

"Did I think when I came out of high school that I'd be a bench player in my junior year? No," he said, being refreshingly honest. "But I don't think anybody could have foreseen what happened to me these last few years."

Which is why he wanted to savor every little moment on the trip to the Final Four, because he knew what it was like as an outsider.

Blue-collar champions

BY DREW SHARP

Flint, a decaying auto town, is the picture of urban squalor — plywood-covered windows, endless rows of vacant buildings. But there is pride stamped on the arms of an increasing number of local teenagers.

"Anytime you go around the city, you see a lot of kids wearing their Flint tattoos," said Flint Northwestern junior Kelvin Torbert, one of the top high school basketball players in the country. "Or the hot one now is getting a Fred Flintstone face on your arm. And all they talk about is going to play for Michigan State when they get older. They want to be a Flintstone."

And that might include Torbert. He hasn't gotten his tattoo yet, but he concedes that it's probably just a matter of time.

"What the Flintstones have done is tell people that there's a lot more to Flint than crime and unemployment," Torbert said. "We're proud of the basketball players who have come from here."

And Tom Izzo seems to have exclusive rights to that pipeline.

Back when Chris Webber, Jalen Rose, Juwan Howard and company made baggy shorts and black socks chic, many assumed the Fab Five would have far-reaching ramifications at Michigan. But the only championship in the years since the Fab Five bolted was one Big Ten conference tournament.

But the marriage between Michigan State and Flint basketball could bear fruit long after the last of the original Flintstones — Charlie Bell — leaves in 2001.

"It's really amazing when you think about the impact that we've had on a city," Bell said. "And every time I see another kid with a Flint tattoo, I know we're having a positive effect on him. They're always coming up to me or Mateen or MoPete and telling us how they're going to keep the tradition

DAVID P. GILKEY

MATEEN CLEAVES (ABOVE) AND MORRIS PETERSON LEFT AN INDELIBLE MARK ON THE MSU PROGRAM.

going. I think that's great."

But the imprint they're leaving is more than basketball. It's about elevating self-esteem and establishing a sense of community and camaraderie.

Following the last home game of the season, three of the mother Stones — Frances Cleaves, Valarie Peterson and Belle Bell — wanted to take a group picture with Izzo as a present for the coach. Izzo joked that if they really wanted to give him a gift, they each could provide him with another tough-as-stone son.

But the mothers assured Izzo that they wouldn't leave the program just because their kids are leaving. They're already working on pitching Michigan State to the next generation of Flintstones — like Torbert.

"This isn't the end, this is just the beginning.
Flint is about strong family roots, and that's what Izzo's building with this program."
FRANCES CLEAVES, MATEEN'S MOTHER

DAVID P. GILKEY

FLINT'S FAVORITE SONS, (FROM LEFT) CHARLIE BELL, MORRIS PETERSON AND MATEEN CLEAVES, ENTER THE RCA DOME.

"This isn't the end, this is just the beginning," Frances Cleaves said. "Flint is about strong family roots, and that's what Izzo's building with this program. Mrs. Peterson and I are still planning on traveling with the team next year, and we want to help the mothers of the new Flint kids here adapt. This could be a new kind of assembly line for Flint, with MSU being GM."

The city's Berston Fieldhouse is to Flint what St. Cecilia's is to Detroit. If you've got game, this is where you get your sternest test. All you see around there is green-and-white jerseys bearing Cleaves' No. 12 or Peterson's No. 42.

"The success of this program is connected to attracting the Flint guys," said Mateen's father, Herbert Cleaves, who does social work for the Flint public schools. "And they're winning because they're tough. Coming back in the final five minutes of a basketball game doesn't scare these kids with the stuff they had to overcome on the streets. That's something that translates positively to the young kids in Flint, and that's what the tattoos are all about. They don't have to be ashamed of telling people where they're from."

High school heroes

BY MICK McCABE

Morris Peterson, Mateen Cleaves and Charlie Bell blossomed on the basketball courts of Flint, nurturing their games and their desire to win.

Peterson was a Free Press dream team all-stater. Antonio Smith, whose MSU career ended in 1999, and Cleaves led Northern to a Class A title.

Flint Northwestern coach Grover Kirkland said he knew Peterson was special but understood why it took everyone else awhile to realize the same thing.

"Up here you had Terrance Roberson at (Saginaw) Buena Vista, and Northern had Antonio and Mateen," Kirkland said. "Pete was just coming into his own."

Peterson blossomed in his senior season and continued to improve after he went to MSU, where he spent a year on the sidelines as a redshirt.

"A big thing helping him was that whenever he complained, he had his mom and dad on his case," Kirkland said.

Saginaw High coach Marshall Thomas is mildly surprised to see Peterson reach the heights he has attained as a Spartan.

"He could always shoot it, but he didn't have the tenacity and the get-up-and-go that he has now," Thomas said. "I don't think he had a lot of confidence in his ability. In high school he was kind of timid.

"His mom and dad were kind of hard on him. I used to talk to his daddy all of the time, and his daddy said he had to become tougher."

No one ever said that about Cleaves, who had been a rugged competitor since his freshman year at Northern.

"Mateen had this success written all over him," Thomas said. "He's

doing now what he did in high school. He willed his team to win. I remember shaking my head and saying, 'What do they expect us to do against him?'

"He had the two big Smith brothers (Antonio and Robaire) on his team, and we used to try to get them outside. But then they threw alley-oop passes to Mateen. I would think, 'This doesn't make sense.' "

Cleaves, a point guard, led Northern to the Class A state title as a junior in 1995, but his team struggled when he was a senior. And he never accepted losing.

"We beat them when we played them as a senior," Kirkland said. "Mateen would come up in tears and tell me: 'We'll get you next time, Coach.' "

Kirkland remembers Cleaves almost beating Northwestern by himself his senior year.

"They were down three with three seconds left," Kirkland said. "Mateen let the ball roll from one end to the other, picked it up and hit a three-pointer to send the game into overtime. I jumped all over my guys for not stopping that."

Cleaves was an all-state quarterback/defensive back in football, so he wasn't afraid of contact.

"His strength was the best part of his game," Flint Central coach Stan Gooch said. "He would go in and handle the big guys if he had to. He was not known as a good shooter in high school, but he had all of the intangibles you can't see."

Bell was an all-stater who scored 2,252 points for Flint Southwestern Academy, more than any other player in Flint history. Unlike some big scorers, he scored a lot against the best teams.

"Our thing was, how are we going to hold him under 45?" Gooch said. "He came in during an era where he was their whole show, and he was still

CLASS OF '95

MORRIS PETERSON
FLINT NORTHWESTERN

CLASS OF '96

MATEEN CLEAVES
FLINT NORTHERN

CLASS OF '97

CHARLIE BELL
FLINT SOUTHWESTERN

MORRIS PETERSON OF
FLINT NORTHWESTERN
MAKES A MOVE TO THE
BASKET IN A GAME
AGAINST FLINT CENTRAL
IN 1995. ACCORDING TO
SAGINAW COACH
MARSHALL THOMAS,
PETERSON WAS A GOOD
SHOOTER WHO LACKED
THE TENACITY HE NOW
SHOWS.

JANE HALE/Flint Journal

ALAN R. KAMUDA

ABOVE: CHARLIE BELL FINISHED HIS
STELLAR HIGH SCHOOL CAREER AT FLINT
SOUTHWESTERN WITH A 10-POINT PER-
FORMANCE AT MAGIC JOHNSON'S ALL-
STAR GAME. RIGHT: DETROIT PERSHING'S
WINFRED WALTON TRIES TO STOP
MATEEN CLEAVES' DRIVE TO THE BASKET
DURING FLINT NORTHERN'S VICTORY IN
THE 1995 CLASS A STATE TITLE GAME.

ALAN R. KAMUDA

very hard to stop. He ran cross-coun-
try, so he would be in tip-top shape.
With his kind of quickness and reac-
tions, he would have been a great
wide receiver or defensive back."

Bell attended Kirkland's summer
camp and was the most valuable
player as a seventh- and eighth-grad-
er.

"His freshman year, this little guy
came out and got 38 points on us,
and I didn't realize it was him,"
Kirkland said. "He scored over 2,000
points, and that's a lot of points for
the Saginaw Valley. We're kind of like
the Big Ten, we just don't allow guys
to score like that.

"He wasn't the best defensive
player in high school, but he was so
quick and so strong. Once he got to
State, they taught him to play
defense."

The success Bell has enjoyed at
MSU was hard to predict because he
was a 6-foot-3 power forward in high
school, and many of his baskets came
in transition.

But like Cleaves and Peterson,
Bell had something inside him that
didn't register on any scouting
report.

"I have not played against anyone
in high school, including Cleaves,
who played as hard as Charlie,"
Thomas said. "He played as hard as
it took to win.

"The thing I liked best was his
work ethic. He never played man-to-
man in high school, but for him to
come along as quickly as he did in
college speaks volumes about him."

Loved ones were the No. 1 fans

A.J. GRANGER DREW ON THE SUPPORT OF HIS FIANCEE, HEATHER WILHELM (LEFT), AND HIS MOTHER, DAWN GRANGER, WHO WERE A PART OF SENIOR DAY FESTIVITIES MARCH 4 AT THE BRESLIN CENTER.

JULIAN H. GONZALEZ

BY JEMELE HILL

The Michigan State contingent began calculating the mileage as soon as the Spartans were named the Midwest Regional's No. 1 seed. Three hours to Cleveland. Thirty or 40 minutes to Auburn Hills. And Indianapolis was a four- or five-hour drive.

A loud cheer broke out in the players' lounge at the United Center in Chicago, where the Spartans watched the NCAA tournament seedings after winning the Big Ten tournament. Cheering hardest were relatives of players, who have, over the years, endured seven-hour drives, lengthy bus rides and expensive airline flights and hotel stays to watch the Spartans play.

"I was relieved," said Herbert Cleaves, Mateen's father. "I didn't have to think about being in debt after it was over with, like last year."

The parents of the Michigan State players don't get any freebies — no free flights, hotel rooms or travel packages. At most, the school could reserve a block of hotel rooms for them, but there were no discounts.

In 1999, the bracket wasn't so kind. There was Milwaukee, St. Louis and finally St. Petersburg. That's one reason Tom Izzo immediately said, "I'm just happy for the families," after the 2000 bracket was announced.

"I'm traveling off my pension checks," said Frances Cleaves, Mateen's mother, a retired autoworker. "I get my check and

send it to the travel agent. I don't even remember how many times I had to fly, what the buses cost me. I know I keep my bank account empty."

In Indianapolis, the families stayed in the same hotel as the players because the school was able to reserve a block of rooms.

"We wanted to be with our families," A. J. Granger said. "I think we tried to be closer to the arena, but they would only give us 25 rooms. We booked out here because of more rooms."

Herbert Cleaves didn't attend the Big Ten tournament in Chicago because, he said, "I was broke. For Florida, I owed everybody in town when I came back. The NCAA has no sympathy for parents."

FROM 64 TO MSU

EAST

- 1. Duke 82
- 16. Lamar 55
- 8. Kansas 81
- 9. De Paul 77 (OT)
- 5. Florida 69
- 12. Butler 68 (OT)
- 4. Illinois 68
- 13. Penn 58
- 6. Indiana 57
- 11. Pepperdine 77
- 3. Oklahoma St. 86
- 14. Hofstra 66
- 7. Oregon 71 (OT)
- 10. Seton Hall 72
- 2. Temple 73
- 15. Lafayette 47

Duke 69 / Kansas 64 → Duke 78
Florida 93 / Illinois 76 → Florida 87
Duke 78 / Florida 87 → Florida 77

Pepperdine 67 / Oklahoma St. 75 → Okla. St. 68
Seton Hall 67 / Temple 65 (OT) → Seton Hall 66
Okla. St. 68 / Seton Hall 66 → Okla. St. 65

Florida 77 / Okla. St. 65 → Florida

MIDWEST

- 1. Michigan St. 65
- 16. Valparaiso 38
- 8. Utah 48
- 9. St. Louis 45
- 5. Kentucky 85
- 12. St. Bon. 80 (2OT)
- 4. Syracuse 79
- 13. Samford 65
- 6. UCLA 65
- 11. Ball State 57
- 3. Maryland 74
- 14. Iona 59
- 7. Auburn 72
- 10. Creighton 69
- 2. Iowa State 88
- 15. Cent. Conn. St. 78

Michigan St. 73 / Utah 61 → Michigan St. 75
Kentucky 50 / Syracuse 52 → Syracuse 58
Michigan St. 75 / Syracuse 58 → Michigan St. 75

UCLA 105 / Maryland 70 → UCLA 56
Auburn 60 / Iowa State 79 → Iowa State 80
UCLA 56 / Iowa State 80 → Iowa State 64

Michigan St. 75 / Iowa State 64 → Michigan St.

Final

Michigan St. 53 / Wisconsin 41 → Michigan St. 89
Florida 71 / North Carolina 59 → Florida 76
Michigan St. 89 / Florida 76 → Michigan St.

Florida / Michigan St.

SOUTH

- 1. Stanford 84
- 16. S. Carolina St. 65
- 8. North Carolina 84
- 9. Missouri 70
- 5. Connecticut 75
- 12. Utah State 67
- 4. Tennessee 63
- 13. La.-Lafayette 58
- 6. Miami (Fla.) 75
- 11. Arkansas 71
- 3. Ohio State 87
- 14. Appalachian St. 61
- 7. Tulsa 89
- 10. UNLV 62
- 2. Cincinnati 64
- 15. NC-Wilmington 47

Stanford 53 / North Carolina 60 → N. Carolina 74
Connecticut 51 / Tennessee 65 → Tennessee 69
N. Carolina 74 / Tennessee 69 → N. Carolina 59

Miami (Fla.) 75 / Ohio State 62 → Miami (Fla.) 71
Tulsa 69 / Cincinnati 61 → Tulsa 80
Miami (Fla.) 71 / Tulsa 80 → Tulsa 55

N. Carolina 59 / Tulsa 55 → North Carolina

WEST

- 1. Arizona 71
- 16. Jackson St. 47
- 8. Wisconsin 66
- 9. Fresno St. 56
- 5. Texas 77
- 12. Indiana St. 61
- 4. LSU 64
- 13. SE Missouri St. 61
- 6. Purdue 62
- 11. Dayton 61
- 3. Oklahoma 74
- 14. Winthrop 50
- 7. Louisville 66
- 10. Gonzaga 77
- 2. St. John's 61
- 15. Northern Ariz. 56

Arizona 59 / Wisconsin 66 → Wisconsin 61
Texas 67 / LSU 72 → LSU 48
Wisconsin 61 / LSU 48 → Wisconsin 64

Purdue 66 / Oklahoma 62 → Purdue 75
Gonzaga 82 / St. John's 76 → Gonzaga 66
Purdue 75 / Gonzaga 66 → Purdue 60

Wisconsin 64 / Purdue 60 → Wisconsin

North Carolina / Wisconsin

ROAD TO INDY

EXHIBITION 1
MSU 115
CALIFORNIA MIDWEST ALL-STARS 66
Friday, Nov. 5, 1999
Breslin Center
Sparty leaders: Jason Richardson — 25 points, 6 rebounds, 2 blocks; Aloysius Anagonye — 12 points, 10 rebounds, 3 blocks.

EXHIBITION 2
MSU 79
MEXICO ALL-STARS 69
Tuesday, Nov. 16, 1999
Breslin Center
Sparty leaders: Morris Peterson — 18 points (13 in second half); Charlie Bell — 12 points, 7 rebounds, 7 assists; Jason Richardson — 12 points, 8 rebounds.
Rank: 2nd.

1-0
MSU 78
TOLEDO 33
Monday, Nov. 22, 1999
Breslin Center
Sparty leaders: Morris Peterson — 19 points, 10 rebounds; Andre Hutson — 15 points, 10 rebounds; Charlie Bell — 11 points.
Rank: 3rd.

2-0
MSU 82
PROVIDENCE 58
Thursday, Nov. 25, 1999
Puerto Rico Shootout
Bayamon, Puerto Rico
Sparty leaders: Morris Peterson — 18 points (5-of-7 shooting, 2-of-2 on three-pointers); Charlie Bell — 15 points, 8 assists, 2 blocks; Mike Chappell — 14 points.
Rank: 3rd.

3-0
MSU 59
SOUTH CAROLINA 56
Friday, Nov. 26, 1999
Puerto Rico Shootout
Bayamon, Puerto Rico
Sparty leaders: Morris Peterson — 21 points (15 in first half); Charlie Bell — 13 points; Andre Hutson — 12 points, 6 rebounds.
Rank: 3rd.

3-1
TEXAS 81
MSU 74
Saturday, Nov. 27, 1999
Puerto Rico Shootout final
Bayamon, Puerto Rico
Sparty leaders: Andre Hutson — 17 points; Morris Peterson — 14 points (back-to-back three-pointers that cut deficit to 76-74 with :49 left).
Rank: 3rd.

4-1
MSU 86
NORTH CAROLINA 76
Wednesday, Dec. 1, 1999
Dean Smith Center,
Chapel Hill, N. C.
Sparty leaders: Morris Peterson — career-high 31 points (12-of-18 shooting, 4-for-6 on three-pointers), 5 steals; Mike Chappell — 13 points; A. J. Granger — 11 points (3-for-4 on three-pointers); Andre Hutson — 10 points, 10 rebounds.
Rank: 8th.

5-1
MSU 75
HOWARD 45
Friday, Dec. 3, 1999
Spartan Classic
Breslin Center
Sparty leaders: Jason Richardson — 16 points; Andre Hutson — 14 points, 10 rebounds; Morris Peterson — 13 points; Charlie Bell — 11 points, 9 rebounds, 4 assists.
Rank: 8th.

6-1
MSU 74
EASTERN MICHIGAN 57
Saturday, Dec. 4, 1999
Spartan Classic final
Breslin Center
Sparty leaders: Morris Peterson — 16 points; Andre Hutson — 15 points (13 in first half, 9-of-9 free throw shooting); Charlie Bell — 11 points; David Thomas — 6 assists.
Rank: 8th.

7-1
MSU 66
KANSAS 54
Tuesday, Dec. 7, 1999
United Center
Chicago
Sparty leaders: Charlie Bell — 21 points (13 on 6-of-8 shooting in the first half); A. J. Granger — 13 points (11 in the first half; 3-of-5 on three-pointers), 9 rebounds, 3 blocks; Morris Peterson — 10 points, 10 rebounds.
Rank: 4th.

7-2
ARIZONA 79
MSU 68
Saturday, Dec. 11, 1999
McKale Center
Tucson, Ariz.
Sparty leaders: Charlie Bell — 20 points; Morris Peterson — 17 points (15 in the second half).
Rank: 4th.

8-2
MSU 86
OAKLAND 51
Saturday, Dec. 18, 1999
Breslin Center
Sparty leaders: Charlie Bell — 20 points off the bench (7-of-9 shooting); Mike Chappell — college career-high 19 points (10 during a 22-5 first-half run), 6 rebounds.
Rank: 5th.

8-3
KENTUCKY 60
MSU 58
Thursday, Dec. 23, 1999
Adolph Rupp Arena
Lexington, Ky.
Sparty leaders: Morris Peterson — 18 points. Jason Richardson — 9 rebounds.
Rank: 5th.

9-3
MSU 96
MISSISSIPPI VALLEY STATE 63
Tuesday, Dec. 28, 1999
Breslin Center
Sparty leaders: Morris Peterson — 22 points (4-of-7 on three-pointers), 8 rebounds; Andre Hutson — season-high 19 points; Mike Chappell — 18 points; Charlie Bell — 11 assists.
Rank: 8th.

JULIAN H. GONZALEZ

THE GOOD NEWS FROM THE MIDWEST REGIONAL FINAL MADE FOR A BANNER HEADLINE AT THE PALACE.

9-4
WRIGHT STATE 53
MSU 49
Thursday, Dec. 30, 1999
Nutter Center
Dayton, Ohio
Sparty leaders: A. J. Granger — 17 points, 2 blocks; Mike Chappell — 10 points.
Rank: 8th.

10-4
MSU 76
PENN STATE 63
Wednesday, Jan. 5, 2000
Breslin Center
Sparty leaders: A.J. Granger — 15 points; Charlie Bell — 14 points; Mateen Cleaves (season debut) — 8 points, 5 assists in 21 minutes.
Rank: 11th.

11-4
MSU 75
IOWA 53
Saturday, Jan. 8, 2000
Carver-Hawkeye Arena
Iowa City, Iowa
Sparty leaders: Morris Peterson — 29 points (20 in the first half; 4 three-pointers in the first 20 minutes), 8 rebounds, 4 assists; Andre Hutson — 14 points; Charlie Bell — 7 assists.
Rank: 11th.

12-4
MSU 77
INDIANA 71 (OT)
Tuesday, Jan. 11, 2000
Breslin Center
Sparty leaders: Charlie Bell — 22 points, 4 steals, 2 blocks; Morris Peterson — 17 points (forced OT with three-pointer with 11.3 seconds left); A. J. Granger — 13 points, 8 rebounds, 2 blocks, 2 steals; Mateen Cleaves — 8 assists.
Rank: 11th.

12-5
OHIO STATE 78
MSU 67
Thursday, Jan. 20, 2000
Value City Arena
Columbus, Ohio
Sparty leaders: Morris Peterson — 20 points; Andre Hutson — 14 points; Mateen Cleaves — 10 points, 7 assists.
Rank: 10th.

13-5
MSU 69
NORTHWESTERN 45
Saturday, Jan. 22, 2000
Breslin Center
Sparty leaders: Charlie Bell — 14 points; Morris Peterson — 11 points (7 during 14-0 opening run), 8 rebounds; Andre Hutson — 11 points, 8 rebounds; Aloysius Anagonye — 8 rebounds.
Rank: 10th.

14-5
MSU 59
NORTHWESTERN 29
Thursday, Jan. 27, 2000
Welsh-Ryan Arena
Evanston, Ill.
Sparty leaders: Morris Peterson — 19 points (9 in the first 10 minutes); Mateen Cleaves — 9 assists, 7 points; Andre Hutson — 10 rebounds; Aloysius Anagonye — 3 blocks.
Rank: 9th.

15-5
MSU 91
ILLINOIS 66
Sunday, Jan. 30, 2000
Breslin Center
Sparty leaders: Mateen Cleaves — 13 points, 12 assists, 4 steals; Charlie Bell — 20 points; Morris Peterson — 18 points (5-of-7 on three-pointers); Andre Hutson — 14 points, career-high 11 rebounds.
Rank: 9th.

16-5
MSU 82
MICHIGAN 62
Tuesday, Feb. 1, 2000
Crisler Arena
Sparty leaders: Morris Peterson — career-high 32 points (11-of-15 shooting, 5-of-8 on three-pointers), 10 rebounds; Mateen Cleaves — 19 points; Andre Hutson — 10 points, 10 rebounds (9 in the first eight minutes).
Rank: 8th.

17-5
MSU 85
CONNECTICUT 66
Saturday, Feb. 5, 2000
Breslin Center
Sparty leaders: Morris Peterson —
16 points; Jason Richardson —
14 points, 7 rebounds;
A. J. Granger — 13 points, 8
rebounds; Charlie Bell — 11
points (3-of-5 on three-pointers),
4 steals.
Rank: 8th.

17-6
PURDUE 70
MSU 67
Tuesday, Feb. 8, 2000
Mackey Arena,
West Lafayette, Ind.
Sparty leaders: A. J. Granger —
17 points, 12 rebounds; Mateen
Cleaves — 11 points, 9 assists.
Rank: 6th.

18-6
MSU 61
WISCONSIN 44
Saturday, Feb. 12, 2000
Kohl Center
Madison, Wis.
Sparty leaders: Morris Peterson —
18 points (2-of-3 on three-
pointers), 10 rebounds; A. J.
Granger — 11 points (3-of-5 on
three-pointers), 11 rebounds.
Rank: 6th.

19-6
MSU 83
OHIO STATE 72
Tuesday, Feb. 15, 2000
Breslin Center
Sparty leaders: Morris Peterson —
26 points, 11 rebounds; Mateen
Cleaves — 24 points (3-of-4 on
three-pointers), 7 assists;
Charlie Bell — 23 points
(14 in second half, including
6 of MSU's first 8).
Rank: 6th.

THE SPARTANS' 75-58 VICTORY
OVER SYRACUSE FEATURED A
RIVETING COMEBACK AND SENT
MATEEN CLEAVES INTO A
TRIUMPHANT SPRINT ON THE
PALACE FLOOR.

JULIAN H. GONZALEZ

20-6
MSU 59
WISCONSIN 54
Saturday, Feb. 19, 2000
Breslin Center
Sparty leaders: Morris Peterson — 15 points; Charlie Bell — 15 points; Mateen Cleaves — 12 points (5 down the stretch), 6 assists.
Rank: 6th.

21-6
MSU 79
PENN STATE 63
Wednesday, Feb. 23, 2000
Bryce Jordan Center,
State College, Pa.
Sparty leaders: Morris Peterson — 17 points; Mateen Cleaves — 11 points, 10 assists; Charlie Bell — 11 points; A. J. Granger — 15 points, 8 rebounds; David Thomas — 10 rebounds.
Rank: 5th.

21-7
INDIANA 81
MSU 79 (OT)
Saturday, Feb. 26, 2000
Assembly Hall,
Bloomington, Ind.
Sparty leaders: Mateen Cleaves — 22 points; Andre Hutson — 17 points; Charlie Bell — 13 points, 7 rebounds; Morris Peterson — 11 points, 10 rebounds.
Rank: 5th.

22-7
MSU 79
MINNESOTA 43
Thursday, March 2, 2000
Breslin Center
Sparty leaders: Mike Chappell — 18 points; Morris Peterson — 13 points; Mateen Cleaves — 12 points, 9 assists; Charlie Bell —11 points; Jason Richardson —12 rebounds.
Rank: 7th.

23-7
MSU 114
MICHIGAN 63
Saturday, March 4, 2000
Breslin Center
Sparty leaders: Mateen Cleaves — 20 assists (Big Ten single-game record); Charlie Bell — career-high 31 points (13-of-19 shooting, 4-of-6 on three-pointers), 4 steals; A. J. Granger — 18 points (7-of-8 shooting, 4-of-4 on three-pointers); Andre Hutson — 15 points, 3 steals; Jason Richardson — 13 points; Morris Peterson — 12 points.
Rank: 7th.

24-7
MSU 75
IOWA 65
Friday, March 10, 2000
Big Ten tournament
United Center, Chicago
Sparty leaders: Morris Peterson 22 points (5 straight early in the second half; 4-of-6 on three-pointers), 9 rebounds; Charlie Bell — 16 points, 6 assists; Mateen Cleaves — 14 points, 7 assists; A. J. Granger — 10 points, 9 rebounds.
Rank: 5th.

25-7
MSU 55
WISCONSIN 46
Saturday, March 11, 2000
Big Ten tournament
United Center, Chicago
Sparty leaders: Morris Peterson — 18 points; Mateen Cleaves — 13 points, 7 assists; Andre Hutson — 10 points (6 straight in the first half), 8 rebounds.
Rank: 5th.

26-7
MSU 76
ILLINOIS 61
Sunday, March 12, 2000
Big Ten tournament final
United Center, Chicago
Sparty leaders: A. J. Granger — 17 points (10 in the first half); Morris Peterson — 14 points; Andre Hutson — 14 points; Mateen Cleaves — 12 points (after missing first 6 shots), 6 assists.
Rank: 5th.

27-7
MSU 65
VALPARAISO 38
Thursday, March 16, 2000
NCAA first round,
Cleveland State Convocation Center
Sparty leaders: Mateen Cleaves — 15 points, 8 assists; Morris Peterson — 12 points; Jason Richardson — 10 rebounds, 9 points; Adam Ballinger — 8 points, 3 rebounds.
Rank: 2nd.

28-7
MSU 73
UTAH 61
Saturday, March 18, 2000
NCAA second round,
Cleveland State Convocation Center
Sparty leaders: Mateen Cleaves — 21 points (13 in the second half); Andre Hutson — 19 points, 8 rebounds; Morris Peterson — 13 points (3-of-4 on three-pointers).
Rank: 2nd.

29-7
MSU 75
SYRACUSE 58
Thursday, March 23, 2000
NCAA Midwest Regional semifinal,
Palace
Sparty leaders: Morris Peterson — 21 points (5-of-9 on three-pointers); A. J. Granger — career-high 19 points (7-of-11 shooting), 2 blocks; Charlie Bell — 12 points, 6 rebounds; Andre Hutson — 11 points, 5 rebounds.
Rank: 2nd.

30-7
MSU 75
IOWA STATE 64
Saturday, March 25, 2000
NCAA Midwest Regional final,
Palace
Sparty leaders: Morris Peterson — 18 points (13 in the second half; 7-of-7 free throws), 7 rebounds; A. J. Granger — 18 points (6-of-6 free throws); Andre Hutson — 17 points (9 straight as MSU narrowed deficit to 48-47; 5-of-5 free throws), 11 rebounds (9 defensive); Mateen Cleaves — 10 points, 2 blocks.
Rank: 2nd.

31-7
MSU 53
WISCONSIN 41
Saturday, April 1, 2000
NCAA semifinal
RCA Dome, Indianapolis
Sparty leaders: Morris Peterson — 20 points (16 in the second half, including 10 during a 13-2 run that pushed a two-point halftime lead to 32-19); 7-of-15 from the floor, 7 rebounds; Mateen Cleaves — 11 points (9-of-11 free throws); Andre Hutson — 10 points (4-of-5 free throws), 10 rebounds (six on offensive glass); Charlie Bell — 8 rebounds; Mike Chappell — 5 points in 9 minutes.
Rank: 2nd.

32-7
MSU 89
FLORIDA 76
Monday, April 3, 2000
NCAA championship
RCA Dome, Indianapolis
Sparty leaders: Morris Peterson — 21 points, 5 assists; A. J. Granger — 19 points (7-of-11 shooting), 9 rebounds; Mateen Cleaves — 18 points (7-of-11 shooting); Charlie Bell — 9 points, 8 rebounds, 5 assists; Jason Richardson — 9 points.
Rank: 2nd.

MSU 65, VALPARAISO 38
Thursday, March 16, 2000
NCAA first round – Cleveland

VALPARAISO CRUSADERS (19-13)

	min	fg	ft	reb o-t	a	pf	pts
Toatley	26	1-7	0-0	1-3	1	3	2
Barton	31	4-12	2-2	3-7	1	4	13
Nuness	22	1-3	0-0	0-2	0	1	3
Grafs	27	2-6	3-4	3-8	2	3	7
Jenkins	22	0-5	0-0	0-3	0	1	0
Stovall	31	1-8	1-2	1-1	1	1	4
Vujic	23	3-8	0-0	0-4	1	3	6
Price	11	1-3	1-2	0-1	0	1	3
Thomason	5	0-0	0-0	0-0	0	1	0
Nikkila	2	0-0	0-0	0-0	0	0	0
Totals	**200**	**13-52**	**7-10**	**8-29**	**6**	**18**	**38**

3PG: 5-23, .217 (Barton 3-7, Nuness 1-3, Stovall 1-5, Toatley 0-2, Price 0-2, Jenkins 0-4). FG .250, FT .700. Team rebounds: 2. Blocks: 2 (Vujic 2). Turnovers: 13 (Vujic 5, Toatley 2, Stovall 2, Barton, Grafs, Price, Thomason). Steals: 4 (Toatley 2, Barton, Grafs).

MICHIGAN STATE SPARTANS (27-7)

	min	fg	ft	o-t	a	pf	pts
Cleaves	32	5-11	3-3	0-2	8	0	15
Bell	16	0-3	0-0	0-4	1	3	0
Hutson	21	1-3	2-2	0-4	2	4	4
Peterson	27	5-9	1-1	0-4	0	0	12
Granger	29	3-5	0-0	1-3	1	1	7
Smith	4	0-1	0-0	0-1	0	0	0
Thomas	7	0-1	1-2	0-2	1	0	1
Chappell	14	2-5	4-6	2-4	0	3	9
Cherry	2	0-0	0-0	0-0	1	0	0
Richardson	25	3-6	2-3	2-10	0	0	9
Anagonye	3	0-0	0-0	0-0	0	1	0
Ballinger	20	3-6	2-2	2-3	0	3	8
Totals	**200**	**22-50**	**15-19**	**7-37**	**14**	**15**	**65**

3PG: 6-17, .353 (Richardson 1-1, Granger 1-2, Cleaves 2-6, Peterson 1-3, Chappell 1-3, Bell 0-2,). FG .440, FT .789. Team rebounds: 2. Blocks: 2 (Granger, Ballinger). Turnovers: 10 (Cleaves 3, Thomas 2, Chappell 2, Bell, Peterson, Smith). Steals: 5 (Thomas 2, Cleaves, Bell, Richardson).

Valparaiso	**15**	**23**	**—**	**38**
Michigan State	**29**	**36**	**—**	**65**

A: 13,374. Officials: Curtis Shaw, Tom Lopes, Olandis Pool.

MSU 73, UTAH 61
Saturday, March 18, 2000
NCAA second round – Cleveland

UTAH UTES (23-9)

	min	fg	ft	reb o-t	a	pf	pts
Harvey	38	7-16	0-1	0-3	6	2	15
Mottola	34	5-10	6-6	1-5	1	4	16
Johnsen	33	2-3	0-0	1-3	2	2	5
Cullen	25	3-7	0-0	0-2	3	2	8
Jensen	36	5-7	1-5	2-5	1	4	13
Colbert	13	0-0	0-0	0-1	2	0	0
Puzey	6	0-1	0-0	0-0	1	3	0
Althoff	15	2-2	0-0	1-2	0	1	4
Totals	**200**	**24-46**	**7-12**	**5-21**	**16**	**18**	**61**

3PG: 6-20, .300 (Jensen 2-4, Johnsen 1-2, Cullen 2-6, Harvey 1-6, Mottola 0-2). FG .522, FT .583. Team rebounds: 0. Blocks: 1 (Mottola). Turnovers: 9 (Mottola 3, Johnsen 3, Harvey, Cullen, Jensen). Steals: 4 (Harvey 2, Johnsen, Cullen).

MICHIGAN STATE SPARTANS (28-7)

	min	fg	ft	o-t	a	pf	pts
Cleaves	36	7-14	3-4	0-2	5	1	21
Bell	31	2-5	5-6	1-5	3	1	9
Hutson	30	7-9	5-10	4-8	2	1	19
Peterson	33	5-11	0-0	1-3	0	2	13
Granger	33	3-5	0-0	0-3	2	2	7
Thomas	8	0-0	0-0	0-1	0	1	0
Chappell	2	0-0	0-0	0-0	0	0	0
Richardson	13	1-2	0-0	2-4	0	4	2
Anagonye	6	1-1	0-0	0-0	1	2	2
Ballinger	8	0-0	0-0	0-0	0	1	0
Totals	**200**	**26-47**	**13-20**	**8-26**	**13**	**15**	**73**

3PG: 8-15, .533 (Peterson 3-4, Cleaves 4-7, Granger 1-3, Bell 0-1). FG .553, FT .650. Team rebounds: 4. Blocks: 1 (Thomas). Turnovers: 10 (Granger 3, Peterson 2, Cleaves, Bell, Hutson, Anagonye, Ballinger). Steals: 3 (Cleaves, Peterson, Granger).

Utah	**35**	**26**	**—**	**61**
Michigan State	**32**	**41**	**—**	**73**

A: 13,374. Officials: Gerald Boudreaux, Mike Thibodeaux, Tom Lopes.

MSU 75, SYRACUSE 58
Thursday, March 23, 2000
NCAA regional semifinal – Palace

SYRACUSE ORANGEMEN (26-6)

	min	fg	ft	reb o-t	a	pf	pts
EThomas	37	3-3	1-2	1-6	0	4	7
Brown	26	4-8	0-0	2-5	0	3	8
Blackwell	37	4-13	1-3	3-6	4	3	9
Bland	8	1-1	0-0	0-0	0	0	3
Hart	40	5-11	0-0	0-3	10	4	11
Shumpert	20	2-6	0-0	0-2	0	2	6
Griffin	32	5-10	4-4	0-1	1	3	14
Totals	**200**	**24-52**	**6-9**	**6-23**	**15**	**19**	**58**

3PG: 4-12, .333 (Shumpert 2-5, Bland 1-1, Hart 1-4, Blackwell 0-1, Griffin 0-1). FG .462, FT .667. Team rebounds: 4. Blocks: 2 (E. Thomas 2). Turnovers: 11 (Hart 4, E. Thomas 3, Griffin 2, Blackwell, Shumpert). Steals: 5 (Hart 3, Griffin, Shumpert).

MICHIGAN STATE SPARTANS (29-7)

	min	fg	ft	o-t	a	pf	pts
Granger	33	7-11	3-3	2-4	3	1	19
Hutson	34	5-7	1-4	2-5	1	2	11
Peterson	34	6-10	4-4	1-3	2	2	21
Cleaves	38	4-12	0-0	0-1	7	1	10
Bell	29	3-7	4-4	1-6	4	1	12
DThomas	2	0-0	0-0	0-1	0	0	0
Chappell	15	0-1	1-2	1-4	0	2	1
Richardson	11	0-1	0-0	0-3	0	0	0
Anagonye	4	0-0	1-2	1-1	0	4	1
Totals	**200**	**25-49**	**14-19**	**8-28**	**17**	**13**	**75**

3PG: 11-23, .478 (Peterson 5-9, Bell 2-4, Granger 2-4, Cleaves 2-6). FG .510, FT .737. Team rebounds: 2. Blocks: 3 (Granger 2, Peterson). Turnovers: 10 (Cleaves 3, Hutson 3, Bell 2, Peterson, D. Thomas). Steals: 3 (Bell, Cleaves, Hutson).

Syracuse	**34**	**24**	**—**	**58**
Michigan State	**24**	**51**	**—**	**75**

A: 21,214. Officials: Scott Thornley, Bob Sitov, Rick Hartzell.

MSU 75, IOWA STATE 64
Saturday, March 25, 2000
NCAA regional final – Palace

IOWA STATE CYCLONES (32-5)

	min	fg	ft	reb o-t	a	pf	pts
Horton	32	1-5	4-4	0-6	2	2	6
Johnson	29	1-1	0-1	2-5	0	0	2
Fizer	36	6-15	2-2	0-4	1	4	15
Tinsley	34	5-13	5-7	1-3	2	4	18
Nurse	40	5-11	2-2	0-4	1	5	17
Hawkins	13	1-2	0-0	3-7	0	2	2
Shirley	16	1-3	2-2	3-4	2	5	4
Totals	**200**	**20-50**	**15-18**	**9-33**	**8**	**22**	**64**

FG: .400. FT: .833. 3PG: 9-26, .346 (Nurse 5-9, Tinsley 3-8, Fizer 1-6, Horton 0-3). Team rebounds: 5. Blockes: 3 (Tinsley 3). Turnovers: 19 (Tinsley 5, Fizer 3, Horton 3, Nurse 3, Johnson 2, Shirley 2, Hawkins). Steals: 1 (Hawkins). Technical fouls: 2 (Bench 2). Ejected: coach Eustachy.

MICHIGAN STATE SPARTANS (30-7)

	min	fg	ft	o-t	a	pf	pts
Hutson	24	6-9	5-5	2-11	2	4	17
Peterson	36	5-13	7-7	3-7	0	3	18
Granger	36	5-8	6-6	0-0	2	2	18
Cleaves	34	4-12	1-2	0-1	2	4	10
Bell	27	3-11	2-2	0-5	2	4	9
Smith	1	0-0	0-0	0-0	0	0	0
Thomas	4	0-0	0-0	0-0	0	1	0
Ishbia	1	0-0	0-0	0-0	0	0	0
Chappell	15	1-2	0-0	1-1	1	0	2
Richardson	13	0-1	0-0	1-2	0	1	0
Anagonye	8	0-0	1-2	0-0	0	4	1
Ballinger	1	0-0	0-0	0-0	0	0	0
Totals	**200**	**24-56**	**22-24**	**7-27**	**9**	**23**	**75**

FG: .429. FT: .917. 3PG: 5-19, .263 (Granger 2-4, Peterson 1-3, Cleaves 1-4, Bell 1-6, Chappell 0-1, Richardson 0-1). Team rebounds: 0. Blocks: 3 (Cleaves 2, Peterson). Turnovers: 8 (Cleaves 5, Bell, Hutson, Peterson). Steals: 6 (Bell 3, Cleaves 2, Peterson). Technical: (bench).

Iowa State	**31**	**33**	**—**	**64**
Michigan State	**34**	**41**	**—**	**75**

A: 21,214. Officials: Curtis Shaw, Frank Basone, Lonnie Dixon.

MSU 53, WISCONSIN 41
Saturday, April 1, 2000
NCAA semifinal – Indianapolis

WISCONSIN BADGERS (22-14)

	min	fg	ft	reb o-t	a	pf	pts
Kowske	20	1-2	0-2	0-0	0	4	2
Kelley	30	1-2	0-0	0-7	3	3	2
Vershaw	31	2-11	1-1	1-2	3	3	5
Bryant	27	1-5	0-0	0-1	1	3	2
Boone	25	6-9	5-6	1-3	0	2	18
Wills	19	1-4	0-0	0-1	0	2	2
Duany	11	0-2	0-0	0-0	0	0	0
Linton	10	0-4	0-0	0-1	1	0	0
Davis	10	1-1	1-2	0-2	0	2	4
Penney	14	2-3	0-0	0-2	0	0	6
Faust	1	0-0	0-0	0-0	0	0	0
R.Smith	1	0-0	0-0	0-0	0	0	0
Swartz	1	0-0	0-0	0-0	0	0	0
Totals	**200**	**15-43**	**7-11**	**2-19**	**8**	**19**	**41**

FG: .349. FT: .636. 3PG: 4-13, .308 (Penney 2-3, Boone 1-1, Davis 1-1, Duany 0-1, Kelley 0-1, Linton 0-1, Vershaw 0-1, Wills 0-1, Bryant 0-3). Team rebounds: 1. Blocks: 4 (Kowske 4). Turnovers: 11 (Boone 5, Bryant 2, Linton 2, Duany, Vershaw). Steals: 2 (Kelley 2).

MICHIGAN STATE SPARTANS (31-7)

	min	fg	ft	o-t	a	pf	pts
Hutson	32	3-7	4-5	6-10	0	2	10
Peterson	33	7-15	4-4	3-7	0	3	20
Granger	32	0-3	1-2	1-7	1	4	1
Cleaves	36	1-7	9-11	0-4	1	3	11
Bell	30	2-9	0-0	2-8	2	2	4
Richardson	10	0-0	0-0	0-0	0	1	0
Anagonye	12	1-1	0-0	1-2	0	2	2
Chappell	9	2-4	1-1	0-0	0	1	5
Ballinger	3	0-0	0-0	0-1	0	0	0
Thomas	3	0-0	0-0	0-0	0	0	0
Totals	**200**	**16-46**	**19-23**	**13-39**	**4**	**18**	**53**

FG: .348. FT: .826. 3PG: 2-14, .143 (Peterson 2-8, Granger 0-1, Chappell 0-2, Bell 0-3). Team rebounds: 3. Blocks: 3 (Chappell 2, Ballinger). Turnovers: 14 (Cleaves 4, Granger 3, Hutson 3, Bell 2, Anagonye, Peterson). Steals: 3 (Cleaves 2, Peterson).

Wisconsin	**17**	**24**	**—**	**41**
Michigan State	**19**	**34**	**—**	**53**

A: 43,116. Officials: John Clougherty, Andre Patillo, Tim Higgins.

MSU 89, FLORIDA 76
Monday, April 3, 2000
NCAA championship – Indianapolis

FLORIDA GATORS (29-9)

	min	fg	ft	reb o-t	a	pf	pts
Wright	29	5-8	3-5	4-10	4	4	13
Miller	31	2-5	5-6	1-3	2	0	10
Haslem	28	10-12	7-7	2-2	0	4	27
Dupay	15	0-4	0-0	0-0	1	2	0
Hamilton	14	0-1	0-0	0-0	0	1	0
Nelson	26	4-10	0-0	1-4	3	1	11
Bonner	7	0-3	0-0	1-3	0	1	0
Weaks	22	1-3	0-0	1-1	1	2	3
Harvey	16	3-11	3-4	4-6	0	2	9
Parker	12	1-3	0-0	0-0	2	2	3
Totals	**200**	**26-60**	**18-22**	**14-29**	**13**	**19**	**76**

3PG: 6-18, .333 (Nelson 3-6, Weaks 1-1, Miller 1-2, Parker 1-3, Hamilton 0-1, Wright 0-1, Bonner 0-2, Dupay 0-2). FG .433, FT .818. Team rebounds: 1. Blocks: 2 (Harvey, Haslem). Turnovers: 13 (Haslem 3, Nelson 3, Harvey 2, Miller 2, Parker, Weaks, Wright). Steals: 5 (Nelson 2, Weaks 2, Wright).

MICHIGAN STATE SPARTANS (32-7)

	min	fg	ft	o-t	a	pf	pts
Hutson	23	2-4	2-2	0-1	3	4	6
Peterson	32	7-14	4-6	1-2	5	3	21
Granger	33	7-11	2-2	2-9	1	2	19
Cleaves	31	7-11	1-1	0-2	4	1	18
Bell	32	3-6	2-3	3-8	5	2	9
Richardson	16	4-7	1-2	1-2	0	1	9
Anagonye	12	0-0	0-0	2-3	0	4	0
Chappell	7	2-4	0-0	1-1	0	0	5
Ballinger	7	1-1	0-0	0-0	0	2	2
Thomas	4	0-0	0-0	1-1	1	1	0
Ishbia	1	0-1	0-0	0-0	0	0	0
Cherry	1	0-0	0-0	0-0	0	0	0
Smith	1	0-1	0-0	0-0	0	0	0
Totals	**200**	**33-59**	**12-16**	**11-29**	**19**	**20**	**89**

3PG: 11-22, .500 (Cleaves 3-4, Granger 3-5, Peterson 3-8, Bell 1-2, Chappell 1-3). FG .559, FT .750. Team rebounds: 3. Blocks: 1 (Anagonye). Turnovers: 14 (Peterson 3, Anagonye 2, Bell 2, Cleaves 2, Granger 2, Chappell, Hutson, Thomas). Steals: 5 (Bell 2, Chappell, Peterson, Richardson).

Florida	**32**	**44**	**—**	**76**
Michigan State	**43**	**46**	**—**	**89**

A: 43,116. Officials: James Burr, Gerald Boudreaux, David Hall.

NO.	PLAYER	POS	HT	WT	YR	HOMETOWN/HIGH SCHOOL
25	Aloysius Anagonye	F	6-8	235	Fr.	Southfield/Detroit DePorres
55	Adam Ballinger	F	6-9	245	Fr.	Bluffton, Ind./Bluffton
14	Charlie Bell	G	6-3	195	Jr.	Flint/Southwestern
20	Mike Chappell	F	6-9	205	Jr.	Southfield/Southfield-Lathrup
22	Steve Cherry	F	6-6	190	Jr.	Coldwater/Coldwater
12	Mateen Cleaves	G	6-2	195	Sr.	Flint/Northern
43	A.J. Granger	F	6-9	230	Sr.	Findlay, Ohio/Liberty-Benton
34	Andre Hutson	F	6-8	240	Jr.	Trotwood, Ohio/Madison
15	Mat Ishbia	G	5-10	155	So.	Bloomfield/Birmingham Seaholm
42	Morris Peterson	F	6-6	215	Sr.	Flint/Northwestern
23	Jason Richardson	G-F	6-6	210	Fr.	Saginaw/Arthur Hill
10	Brandon Smith	G	5-10	165	Jr.	Rochester, N.Y./Sutherland
11	David Thomas	G-F	6-7	205	Jr.	Brampton, Ontario/Notre Dame

Coach: Tom Izzo

SEASON (32-7)

PLAYER	G	FG%	FT%	REB	AST	PTS
Anagonye	34	.556	.630	3.0	0.3	2.9
Ballinger	37	.644	.789	1.7	0.3	2.0
Bell	39	.453	.802	4.9	3.2	11.5
Chappell	39	.383	.729	2.2	0.6	5.9
Cherry	12	.273	—	0.2	0.3	0.7
Cleaves	26	.421	.756	1.8	6.9	12.1
Granger	39	.500	.893	5.3	1.2	9.5
Hutson	39	.586	.669	6.2	1.5	10.2
Ishbia	18	.600	.500	0.2	0.2	0.5
Peterson	39	.465	.773	6.0	1.3	16.8
Richardson	37	.503	.548	4.1	0.6	5.1
Smith	27	.250	.333	0.2	0.8	0.4
Thomas	34	.408	.714	2.4	1.5	2.4
MSU	39	.474	.735	38.9	15.4	74.1
Opp.	39	.394	.683	27.0	11.1	58.9

NCAA TOURNAMENT (6-0)

PLAYER	G	FG%	FT%	REB	AST	PTS
Anagonye	6	1.000	.500	1.2	0.2	1.0
Ballinger	5	.571	1.000	0.8	0.0	2.0
Bell	6	.317	.867	6.0	2.8	7.2
Chappell	6	.438	.667	1.5	0.2	3.7
Cherry	2	—	—	0.0	0.5	0.0
Cleaves	6	.418	.810	2.0	4.5	14.2
Granger	6	.581	.923	4.3	1.7	11.8
Hutson	6	.615	.679	6.5	1.7	11.2
Ishbia	2	.000	—	0.0	0.0	0.0
Peterson	6	.486	.909	4.3	1.2	17.5
Richardson	6	.471	.600	3.5	0.0	3.3
Smith	3	.000	—	0.3	0.0	0.0
Thomas	6	.000	.500	0.8	0.3	0.2
	6	.476	.785	31.5	12.7	71.7
	6	.403	.732	25.8	11.0	56.3

ERIC SEALS

TOM IZZO HAS A HUG AND A FEW WORDS FOR ANDRE HUTSON DURING THE TITLE GAME AGAINST FLORIDA. HUTSON AVERAGED 11.2 POINTS IN THE TOURNAMENT.

CHAMPIONS: TOM IZZO AND MATEEN CLEAVES SHARE TEARS OF JOY.